'What does educational theory *do*? This bold and original text positions educational theory as producer of social realities and political ideas.'

Claudia Ruitenberg, Associate Professor, Philosophy of Education, University of British Columbia, Canada

'Educational theory is seldom treated with more important than it is in this book. Instead of trying to construct yet another educational theory to change, understand or explain the role of education in social contexts, Tomasz Szkudlarek starts from educational theory itself as a porous, vibrating field of energy inherently producing social reality. Instead of social reality establishing the conditions for educational thinking, Szkudlarek stresses how educational theory is a creation of certain visibilities that organize the social world and shape political hegemonies. As such this book is both innovative and provocative in its conceptualisation of the relationship between education, theory and politics and in its capacity to visualise how active social forces constitute what we consider to be 'real'.'

Carl Anders Säfström, Professor of Education, Södertörn University, Sweden

'Tomasz Szkudlarek succeeds superbly in pointing to the constitutive role of education in the construction of the political and in showing why Ernesto Laclau's political theory needs pedagogical supplementation. And while he makes very clear how thinking pedagogically is essentially in need of postulational rhetoric, i.e. in need of using 'should's and 'we's, he at once, brilliantly, makes us become very vigilant about their use. This is a great contribution to educational theory, including truly original readings of the classics Rousseau and Herbart.'

Jan Masschelein, head of the Laboratory for Education and Society, and of the research group Education, Culture and Society, KU Leuven, Belgium

'In this admirably clear, stimulating and path-breaking book Tomasz Szkudlarek politicizes educational theory as a specific genre of public discourse. Through a close engagement with founding figures of educational thought as diverse as Rousseau and Herbart, the author offers valuable explorations of how educational theories are implicated in politics by means of their role in the constitution of social ontology. To this end, Szkudlarek relies on a broad range of important thinkers (from Derrida and Foucault down to Rancière and Laclau) while supplementing their analyses with conceptions that do justice to objections raised by critics. Altogether this important new work brings some much-needed fresh insight to bear on political educational issues of invisible modern power relations and will be welcomed by readers in search of original perspectives on time-honoured tensions within educational and political theory.'

Marianna Papastephanou, Professor, Department of Education, University of Cyprus, Cyprus

On the Politics of Educational Theory

On the Politics of Educational Theory considers the political significance of educational theory as a specific genre of public discourse. Rather than understanding educational theories solely as addressing issues of childrearing and instruction, this book aims to view educational theories in a broader socio-political context. It explores the role of educational theories in the construction of collective and political identities and analyzes them as rhetorical strategies operating as political discourses.

Defining the methodological framework through the perspectives of Michel Foucault and Ernesto Laclau, each chapter examines the ways in which theories of education contribute to the creation of social realities and identities. Such issues as the construction of visibility and invisibility of power, the tropes of temporality, or the use of postulational language where theorists say what "should" be done in and by education, are some of the threads that weave through particular theories – from Rousseau to the discourse of education in the knowledge-based society – analyzed as ontological rhetorics constitutive of political identities.

This book suggests a direction for a more conscious way of dealing with the political in education. As such, it will appeal to researchers, academics, and postgraduate students in the fields of educational research, philosophy of education, curriculum studies, social and political theory, and theory of education.

Tomasz Szkudlarek is Head of the Department of Philosophy of Education and Cultural Studies at the Institute of Education, University of Gdańsk, Poland.

Theorizing Education
Series Editors
Gert Biesta, University of Luxembourg, Luxembourg
Julie Allan, University of Birmingham, UK
Richard Edwards, University of Stirling, UK

Theorizing Education brings together innovative work from a wide range of contexts and traditions which explicitly focuses on the roles of theory in educational research and educational practice. The series includes contextual and socio-historical analyses of existing traditions of theory and theorizing, exemplary use of theory, and empirical work where theory has been used in innovative ways. The distinctive focus for the series is the engagement with educational questions, articulating what explicitly educational function the work of particular forms of theorizing supports.

Books in this series:

For a full list of titles in this series, please visit www.routledge.com

On the Politics of Educational Theory

Rhetoric, theoretical ambiguity, and the construction of society

Tomasz Szkudlarek

Routledge
Taylor & Francis Group

LONDON AND NEW YORK

First published 2017
by Routledge
2 Park Square, Milton Park, Abingdon, Oxon OX14 4RN

and by Routledge
711 Third Avenue, New York, NY 10017

Routledge is an imprint of the Taylor & Francis Group, an informa business

British Library Cataloguing in Publication Data
A catalogue record for this book is available from the British Library

Library of Congress Cataloging-in-Publication Data
Names: Szkudlarek, Tomasz, author.
Title: On the politics of educational theory : rhetoric, theoretical ambiguity and the construction of society / Tomasz Szkudlarek.
Description: New York, NY : Routledge, 2016. | Includes bibliographical references and index.
Identifiers: LCCN 2016022509 | ISBN 9781138890275 (hardback) | ISBN 9781315712505 (ebk)
Subjects: LCSH: Education—Political aspects. | Education—Philosophy. | Education—Aims and objectives. | Education and state—Philosophy.
Classification: LCC LC71 .S968 2016 | DDC 370.1—dc23
LC record available at https://lccn.loc.gov/2016022509

ISBN: 978-1-138-89027-5 (hbk)
ISBN: 978-1-315-71250-5 (ebk)

Typeset in Bembo
by Apex CoVantage, LLC

Printed and bound in Great Britain by
TJ International Ltd, Padstow, Cornwall

Contents

Acknowledgments

I want to express my gratitude to the people and institutions that made the completion of this book possible:

To Gert Biesta, Julie Allan, and Richard Edwards for their inspiration, and for the encouragement to submit the proposal of this book to their "Theorizing Education" series at Routledge;

To the anonymous reviewers of the proposal, whose critical comments helped me to organize the structure of the argument;

To F. Tony Carusi from Massey University, New Zealand, for his supportive and critical comments on the drafts of particular chapters, for friendship, and for inspiration;

To Jennifer Zielińska, Łukasz Tamkun, and the editorial staff at Routledge for their invaluable assistance in the preparation of the book;

And to my wife, Maja Mendel, for the continuous encouragement to finally *write* the book of which we had talked so long, for our discussions at the kitchen table, and for love.

My research was supported by a grant from the National Science Centre (NCN) in Kraków, Poland (grant number 2014/15/B/HS6/03580).

Chapter 1

Theory, (in)visibility, and totality

Theories of education as discourses. By way of introduction

This book does not focus on the political content of educational theories, or on how they describe or design education in relation to the demands of given political systems either overtly, as in the programs of civic education, or covertly, as critical pedagogy aptly reveals. Although I do not exclude such elements from my analyses, they are aspects of a broader issue in which I am interested: the political significance of educational theory as a specific genre of public discourse. The way I understand this perspective is informed by Ernesto Laclau's theory, in which discourse gains ontological meaning: it is constitutive of social structure (Laclau 2005; 2014).[1]

Originally, the notion of discourse refers to linguistic practices (like conversations, policy documents, or media reports), but in Laclau's theory, which deals with the construction of political identities and with the very question of societies *becoming* what they are, discourse is understood in a broader sense:

> Discourse is the primary terrain of the construction of objectivity as such. By discourse ... I do not mean something that is essentially restricted to the area of speech and writing, but any complex of elements in which *relations* play the constitutive role. This means that elements do not pre-exist relational complex but are constituted through it. Thus "relation" and "objectivity" are synonymous.
>
> (Laclau 2005, p. 68)

The broadening of the notion of discourse is helpful in building a theory in which similar structural patterns can be applied to analyze that which falls into the traditionally (linguistically) understood discourse and that which traditionally would be called material conditions. The relations we deal with in social sciences are structured not only by literally understood communication, but by numerous patterns of social space, temporality, and causality; their structures precede objects that can be recognized in given contexts. In other words, the understanding of discourse here is much broader than that applied, for instance, by Jürgen Habermas (1984), for whom the ethics of discourse relates to the process of rational public deliberation constitutive of democratic societies. As

Laclau admits, the source of his understanding of discourse is Foucault's work. In his later publications, however, Laclau redirected this way of thinking about discourse toward a more rhetorical approach and incorporated Lacan's psychoanalytical theory more directly and extensively (Laclau 2005; 2014). His analyses sometimes appear close to Rancière's understanding of politics as well. All these traces will be present in my interpretation of what I call the politics of educational theories.

Educational theories are, thus, analyzed here as ontological devices implicated in the construction of social objectivities. I am interested in how theories are productive of, and how they position themselves in, the flow of signifiers that can be used for the maintenance and change of the social, and how their concepts, explanations, mythologies, and rhetorics can possibly be utilized in other discursive practices which, together, form what Laclau calls political hegemonies, i.e., the figures that give the social its precariously totalized, historically specific shape.[2] What this means in practical terms is that theories are seen not only in their rational and intentional layers: as expert constructions where clearly defined concepts are linked in logical relations so that they form generalized descriptions of given realities in a way that is operational, i.e., that allows for empirical testing, predictions, and the production of technical blueprints. The notion of discourse goes beyond such rational and technological dimensions. It encompasses also that which is vague, contradictory, or figurative; not only descriptions and abstract models, but also persuasion and appeals to identification with their proposed visions; not only logics, but also rhetorics; not only that which is present in them, but also that which is structurally absent; and finally, not only the text, but also the context. Such a broad approach touches a fairly sensitive issue. Theories of education, and the discipline of educational studies in general, are sometimes accused of being dubious in terms of their academic quality, exactly because they are saturated with normative claims and persuasive rhetoric, and because of their notorious lack of conceptual clarity. Seen as discourses, with all these features as constitutive to their genre, along with those believed to be academically solid ones, they can be investigated as implicated in the construction of social ontologies *as they are*, with their scientific and "less scientific" (normative, persuasive, performative, etc.) elements alike. In sum, I try to see theories of education as discourses that "do" something in the space and to the space in which they circulate – not only as representative, but also as performative practices.

Speaking of theories as discourses is not a very common way of analyzing them. When we refer to discourse analysis in educational studies, we usually do so in contexts such as media coverage, policy documents, or classroom interactions. Theories are usually excluded from such discourse-analytical approach; they are *our* cognitive resources, which help us observe, categorize, classify, and connect given phenomena into significant units, and, as such, they usually occupy the position behind our lenses rather than in front of them. To analyze them as connected to other signifying practices in a way that brackets their privilege of transparency and their claims to truth, can be seen as entering the terrain of meta-theoretical work, of aiming toward a theory of theory. While this perspective is attractive for identifying the aim of this book, I would rather avoid some of the connotations of such identification, namely those that stem from the frequent association of the prefix *meta-* with that of *supra-*. The notion of meta-theory tends to evoke a hierarchy of abstraction and generality that inevitably invites the question of the meta-meta-theoretical, and so on, *ad infinitum*. However, the Greek word μετά means "beyond," "upon," or "after," and it does not impart anything more essential or superior to that which it precedes. Such a hierarchical connotation was probably arrived at as an effect of naming (rather accidentally) Aristotle's "first philosophy" as *metaphysics*. To conclude, meta-theory may situate itself beyond theory, at a distance to its language, without necessarily surpassing it "upwards" in the hierarchy of firstness, generality, or abstraction. The discourse-analytical approach which informs my analyses and interpretations does not situate itself above, but rather aside, the theories I am analyzing, and, thus, it creates the possibility of "looking awry" (to use Slavoj Žižek's phrase 1992), in a skewed manner that brings into the focus not only the solid foundations and logical structures built upon them, but also the debris, the abandoned, the provisional, the unintended, the accidental, and the unnecessary as that which is present in the theoretical along with its conceptual constructions. Seeing theories as discourses means, therefore, that they are complex, overdetermined, and porous; they are excessive in their contents and are, at the same time, incomplete, and they involve elements that are alien to their conceptual logic, but are, nevertheless, significant.

I am also interested in the ontological rather than the ontic – in the sense proposed by Ernesto Laclau. The ontological, for Laclau, is social objectivity attainable by discursive and, in particular, by rhetorical means. To that domain Chantal Mouffe (2005) applies the term *the political*, originally coined in 1927 by Carl Schmitt (1996). The difference it makes in terms of the scope and method of the investigation is twofold. First, the contents of theories are seen in a broader context than that of referring to practices of teaching or upbringing isolated from other social actions, and education is seen in relation to how the social, including that which may be called its objectivity, is constructed. Second, it affects the way of seeing the relations between education and politics. I do not mean only how educational theories replicate or conform to the dominant political ideologies, which quite often is the focus in discourse analysis, especially in its critical variety. Such interpretations are insufficient when they conclude with identifying the instances of power in relation to which the analyzed practice appears functional; such conclusions fall easily into a "critical trap," by which I mean certain circularity, which, *if not interpreted further*, may be denounced as a logical error (*petitio principii*). I am referring to cases when we identify a given practice as functional to the dominant structures of power, while these structures, by the very virtue of being dominant, are already known to us as researchers; and, moreover, their hegemony is in fact the very reason why critical analysis has been undertaken. In a way, much of the critical discourse analysis concerning education in late-capitalist societies is somewhat predictable in terms of how it identifies the forces that determine what we do in schools; whatever we choose to investigate can (usually rightly) be concluded with de-masking its implications in neoliberalism, which simply confirms the presuppositions (and often the ethical reasons) on which the very intention of critical analysis was based. This statement sounds like a fundamental critique of critical analysis, and in fact it could be an almost perfect example of *petitio principii*, if the identification of the dominant ideology was indeed the aim of the research. This, however, is not entirely the case. The focus of critical analysis should be, and often is, not on the final de-masking of capitalist plots behind every aspect of social life. Somewhat similar to the work of Freudian psychoanalysis (whatever the analyzed says will be interpreted in terms of her or his sexuality), the issue is not so much to "discover" such a determination as it is to *interpret* it in its particular shape – to dismantle its detailed semantics and mechanics and to re-assemble it into meaningful narratives woven around contingent details so that the whole space is marked with trajectories of their interconnections. Critical thinking would be, in this context, comparable to the hermeneutic of the present; and, as hermeneutical, it should be circular, bi- or multi-directional, as it is in such repetitive circularity that interpretation is possible.

Such hermeneutics are part of the analysis I undertake in this book. They are not intended to de-mask how politics inform the thinking of education. From my point of view, the reverse is equally, if not more, interesting: how does the thinking of education inform the political? How do educational concepts, mythologies, and rhetorics *produce* the resources and the strategies for the political construction of the social? This is not meant to say that I see these foci as competing or contradictory: this is not an either/or issue. I merely want to say that the ontological understanding of discourse, most consequently propagated by Laclau, suggests that one can see education theories as discourses active in construing social realities, as structures and processes the impact of which extends beyond that of being "implemented" in pedagogical practices. Again, the aim here is not to discover such politics of theory, because it is *assumed* on the grounds of discourse theory. The aim is to understand *how* such politics are made.

Let me situate these intentions against the background of the more traditional functions that one can ascribe to theory in education.[3] What I mean here are social and political functions, where theory is set against social practice, rather than those related to empirical research, where theory is seen as related to, and different from, data. The first, and a fairly commonplace, answer implies a technological understanding of the relation between theory and practice; that is, it claims that theory has the task of designing pedagogies and procedures for assessing their efficiency. Another answer refers to the hermeneutic tradition and claims that the need for theory can be understood through the notion of understanding. This implies that the ways we educate are not necessarily derived from prior theoretical statements. Education is a practical thing performed by people who do not have to design their actions before they act. Theory, in this perspective, provides us with languages for reflection, and languages through which we can share these reflections with others, which contributes to mutual understanding. A third, perhaps less common answer, is that theory questions the realities we live in. The abstract language creates distance from the experiential domain. Access to theory makes the world relative, less familiar, and creates a space in which other ways of living and learning are imaginable.

These three uses of theory paraphrase Jürgen Habermas's formulation of the interests that constitute human cognition (Habermas 1972). Management (or technology in a broader sense), reflective understanding, and critique that brings emancipation form an epistemological framework largely consistent with the array of modern political and educational ideologies. These modalities can also be understood, not in terms of competing ideological positions that pit their power against one another, but as momentums in the cycle of human actions as well. We may see them as partial epistemological tools, applicable sequentially – when we do things according to our knowledges; when we realize that what we have done is different from what had been planned and that we need another language to understand it; and when, as a result, the legitimacy of what has been done is questioned. Then we open space for a new design. To sum up, theoretical languages (technological, hermeneutical, and critical) may be seen as functional in relation to different aims, or to different momentums of social praxis in modern societies.

This list of classic functions of theoretical thinking can be fine-tuned and supplemented with observations made by Gert Biesta, Julie Allan, and Richard Edwards (2014). The overarching distinction they make is that between the gestures of bringing "that which is strange and not understood into the domain of understanding" (which encompasses efforts at explanation, hermeneutic understanding, and emancipation), and that of "making the familiar strange," illustrated by Foucault's notion of eventalization that "aims at a breach of self-evidence" (p. 5). In a similar tone, Jacques Rancière (2011) speaks of politics as disruptive of the "distribution of the sensible," and Jean Baudrillard speaks of the radical thought: "The absolute rule of thought is to return the world as we received it: unintelligible. And if it is possible, to return it a little bit more unintelligible. A little bit more enigmatic" (1995, no pagination). The sense of such negative gestures is both in distancing oneself from cognitive and aesthetic "police orders" in Rancière's terms and in opening the space for new articulations. As Thomas Popkewitz (2014) says, theory helps to "unthink" in order to "rethink" the world.

By the very fact of being defined against social practice, all these functions, both in their positive and negative gestures, are political. To say that education is politics (which may imply that politics is education) demands just a small modification of Foucault's claim that knowledge is power as much as power is knowledge (Foucault 1980). The very idea of writing this book started with juxtaposing Foucault's description of modern power with the project of "the science of education" proposed by Johann F. Herbart in 1806 (Herbart 1908). Therefore, in the following section, I reiterate some of the basic tenets of Foucault's understanding of modern power, and then I juxtapose it with Herbart's notion of discipline.

As we know, according to Foucault (1995), the techniques of control established in the advent of modernity (sixteenth to nineteenth centuries) relied on surveillance, and they replaced the former, repressive regimes of power. The paradigmatic figure of that emerging technology is Jeremy Bentham's architectural project of "The Panopticon" (Bentham 1791): the layout of the building makes it possible to observe all its inhabitants (prisoners, workers, patients, students, etc.) in such a way that the observer himself remains invisible. All techniques identified by Foucault as constitutive of modern power relations – hierarchical observation, normalizing judgment, and examination – are dependent on the particular organization of space, which teaches the inhabitants to observe themselves so that they can make rational decisions about their own behavior. Because of the specific organization of visibility in the building, the inmates, not knowing whether they are being observed at a given moment or not, have to concede that they may be being observed all the time. This prompts them to internalize the gaze of the warders and turns them into their own guards. In other words, it turns them into Kantian autonomous subjects capable of seeing themselves through the eyes of the law and of making rational decisions about their behavior. In Kant, moral behavior demands rational thinking, which makes one capable of looking at one's behavior in a de-centered manner, with the eyes of another, namely of the Law. "Act only according to that maxim whereby you can at the same time will that it should become a universal law" (Kant 1993, p. 30). The panoptic mechanism of control invented for the sake of prison reform has spread into other spheres of the public, saturating all places and institutions with its logic. Thus, power becomes fundamentally pedagogical (cf. Ball 1990; Marshall 1996). This feature of modern power relations – the saturation of the social with disciplinary control capable of teaching people to see themselves with the eye of the imagined, normalizing agent – I call *pedagogism* (Szkudlarek 1995; 2003).

This development has had several consequences that are important for the understanding of education. The first is a kind of environmentalism in thinking about the human subject. If architectural design can be granted the power to control human behavior, or, more precisely, to teach people self-control, then deficits in human conduct can be traced back to the faults in the environment itself. The modern examination of the human is developing toward detailed and multidimensional expertise where misdoings and peculiarities of conduct are hypothetically ascribed to external sources, to the stimuli to which the conduct responds (cf. the "border case" of such an examination in Pierre Rivière's trial reported by Foucault 1982). The project of creating autonomous subjects implies, then, that we have to purposefully arrange human environments as formative milieus. A dense network of relevant social and educational institutions is established. Modern knowledge of the human accumulates around such institutions and practices, serving the needs of the emerging political system. The emergence of the humanities and the debate on their scientific status, as well as the establishment of university chairs in pedagogics,[4] psychology, and sociology, may all be related to that development. Gradually, this kind of knowledge is gaining academic status.

What this means is that educational theory emerged during a time when disciplinary control must have been a widespread phenomenon. Johann Friederich Herbart's *Allgemeine Pädagogik . . .*, acclaimed as the first academically sound, modern theory of education, was published in Göttingen in 1806. Herbart does not refer to these apparently widespread developments in disciplinary control; instead he *invents* a similar logic that permits the internalization of government to be the foundation of education. Before we start to analyze this silence about the existing mode of control, with its simultaneous postulating as a desired way of treating children, as instructive about the relation between educational thought and the political construction of modern societies, we need to address the issue of timing. In other words, *how widespread* was disciplinary power in Herbart's times? Could he have missed its presence?

The specificity of the methodology applied in Foucault's research makes it very difficult to judge the scale of the phenomena he is analyzing. He focuses on events, on local practices, and singular institutions, but he never provides sufficient data to answer the question of *when* the transition from punishment to discipline occurred. This process took centuries. For instance, the time span covered by the iconic examples given in *Discipline and Punish* (Foucault 1995) ranges from 1666 to 1843. Moreover, in relation to Foucault's argument, the very "when exactly" question is inadequate: Foucault writes from the position of a spectator immersed within that transition; he works to show how particular practices travel from one place to another, how they are appropriated, rejected or distorted, diffused or concentrated in one place or another. This is a process that runs in many directions simultaneously, and there is no precise measure that could tell us whether the 1806 Europe was already, or was not yet, a disciplinary society. Generally speaking, societies never "are" anything in a way that can identify them as being completely in a certain stage or fix their identity as such and not something else. Nevertheless, the proliferation of disciplinary power, its leaking from enclosed institutions (like cities in the time of plague) to spaces of public visibility, and its transition from being restrictive to being productive, gains density and intensity that allows Foucault to state that the process occupied a *certain* time and place in history:

> The movement from one project to the other, from a scheme of exceptional discipline to one of a generalized surveillance, rests on a historical transformation: the gradual extension of the mechanisms of discipline

throughout the *seventeenth and eighteenth centuries*, their spread throughout *the whole social body*, the formation of what might be called in general the disciplinary society.

(Foucault 1995, p. 209, italics added)

The organization of the police apparatus *in the eighteenth century* sanctioned a generalization of the disciplines that became co-existent with the state itself.

(p. 215, italics added)

The historical research on the emergence of public schooling in Central Europe seems to confirm these statements. As Bernadette Baker says, "The later eighteenth-century *Volksschulen* might be . . . understood . . . as institutions concerned with what Foucault refers to as the 'shepherd-flock game,' in which *formal mechanisms outside of the home were established to inculcate the young with self-monitoring techniques*" (Baker 2001, p. 346, emphasis added).

In short, it seems that during the time Herbart was writing his *Allgemeine Pädagogik*, disciplinary control *was* a widespread phenomenon, not only in prisons, factories, and military barracks, but also in schools and many other institutions. Why, then, does the language of educational reflection developed in that time hardly reflect the proliferation of these techniques of control? As I will argue in Chapter 3, Herbart postulates, or invents, invisible discipline as if it had not existed, at the same time positioning it at the margin of his own theory. This is not a suggestion of some fundamental fault in educational theory; rather, it is a starting point for my attempt at understanding the genre of pedagogical writing. What I mean is that this genre seems to assume the focus on *postulating* (demanding) certain solutions, with not much attention being paid to the description and analysis of those that already exist. Risking a premature generalization, I would say that educational theories either tend to denounce pedagogical arrangements present in the social space, or they treat them selectively, choosing the "proper" ones that they then try to promote, or they ignore them altogether. At the same time, aiming at the propagation of proper education and upbringing, they often call for solutions which are already present in that space. Again, this is not meant to suggest that there is something cognitively or ethically wrong with such a selective description of the present or about postulating things that already exist; it is, again, a starting point for further observations, a possible feature of the genre of pedagogical writing. The moment knowledge of education becomes an academic discipline is interesting. It seems to be productive of an intriguing—and, to date, hardly recognized—relation between the postulates of rational upbringing and schooling, supported by the methodological rigor of scientific investigation, on the one hand, and the formative work of the supposedly commonplace disciplining forces on the other; between rationally designed and academically legitimized pedagogies on the one hand, and the dispersed, silent pedagogism of hierarchical observation, normalizing judgment, and examination on the other. I repeat: the most interesting question, from the perspective of this book, is not one of why educational theory construed itself "in spite" or "against" the existing modes of pedagogism, or whether it is or is not adequate in its representational functions. It is, rather, what it *does* to such practices by way of ignoring them in its descriptive parts and postulating them in its normative claims. In a more general sense, it is about how its discourse operates *in the field* of these practices and how significant it is in relation to their power of construing political realities.

Following Laclau, I try to look at these relations as somewhat constitutive, or, at least, implicated in the construction of social objectivity. This requires that theories are analyzed not only in their narrowly (scientifically) understood conceptual dimensions, but as discourses saturated with rhetorical devices. The intention to analyze not only the logics, but also the rhetorics, of educational theories does not presuppose a kind of uselessness of theory if it is vague, metaphorical, or repetitive in relation to existing structures and practices of pedagogism, but, on the contrary, it initiates a reflection on its possible rhetorical power, on the uses and functionalities which exceed the sphere of technical implementations of scientifically designed pedagogies. In what way can a theory which speaks of things known to the public, and which, moreover, postulates their existence while they already exist, and, as claims Foucault, are widespread and effective, contribute to the social world? Does it not seem excessive or redundant? If the truth value and the innovative value of such a theory can be questionable, what is that "excessive" dimension about? What other uses of such theories are imaginable? Referring to the typology of functions of theory identified by Biesta, Allan, and Edwards (2014), we might suspect that the work of theory in this instance can be seen to be a particular (perhaps distorted) case of the redescription of educational processes, "always already described in some way" (p. 5).

> Although such redescriptions can function as hypotheses and therefore as starting points in empirical work, they do not necessarily and exclusively have to be understood as claims to truth. They can also be seen as possible interpretations of what might be the case – interpretations that can inform teachers' perceptions, judgements and actions by opening up possibilities for seeing things in new and different ways.
>
> (p. 6)

This is a very important statement, but in the context of the aforementioned excessiveness, it calls for another question itself. What happens if such redescriptions reaffirm the commonplace, the already-known? What happens when their critical or innovative value is weak, but they still redescribe the vernacular in lofty, humanistic, or scientific language? Is such a situation of pedagogical or political significance? Or both? In other words, I want to see such possible redescriptions in their political functions – not only as relevant to teachers' work, not even in relation to educational policies, but as elements of public discourse understood in their ontological functions as implicated in the construction of social objectivity. I am, thus, interested in a peculiar *excess of theory* (Szkudlarek 2014), or its supplementarity, in Derridean terms (Derrida 1997), in the genealogy and current transformations of modernity. What I mean here is that educational theories seem to comprise more than is needed for typical functions of scientific description, explanation, and prediction of educational processes; they are saturated with normative statements and are rich in rhetorical tropes, the functions of which have yet to be identified. This implies an assumption that the process of the theorization of education could perform more complex functions than those of solving the technical problems of teaching, promoting understanding of how people learn, or gaining critical distance on how children are turned into adults.

The analysis of educational theories presented in the following chapters gradually "structures itself" around two major dimensions, supplemented with the one of temporality. One of these two follows the Rancièrean understanding of politics through the lens of the sensible, and it is supported by the Foucauldian trait of the role of visibility/invisibility regimes in the construction of modern power. The second is the field of the rhetorical construction of totality, which is inspired by Laclau's theory and supported by Foucault's understanding of discourse. Let me start with an introduction to the issue of visibility and invisibility.

The Foucauldian quest of analyzing modern power through the metaphor of visibility (Bentham's *Panopticon*) translates itself into the question of *how theories organize the visibility and invisibility of social phenomena*. We should start interpreting this question by returning to the ancient tradition. The Greek word *theoria* (θεωρία), like the Latin *contemplatio*, relates to seeing, both in an empirical sense (seeing with one's eyes) and as a mental experience (as in Plato's cave, from which the philosopher ascends to see the light of ideas). Naming conceptual systems as theories brings this connotation to the fore; it is through theory that we make things visible, and we can associate such visibility with both empirical and conceptual domains. Theories help us categorize empirical realities, and – by giving names to things and articulating these names into structures – help us see them as coherently arranged, classified objects of our experience. Theories also make us capable of "seeing" ideas – they build bridges to generalized concepts capable of denoting hierarchically organized classes of objects or of their abstracted (detached) qualities.

One can thus look at theoretical structures as architectural designs of the asymmetry of seeing. As structures of visibility, they must delimit and organize the domain of the invisible as well. It is light that makes the shadow; every concept is set against the background from which it is differentiated, and there are more instances of invisibility that can be identified in this generic sense of theory. One is that of the accidental, or the contingent. We tend do define concepts as essences of things, as that which is necessarily present in every object denoted by the concept. However, no object can be reduced to its essence; every object features that which is particular to the concrete thing and cannot be found in another one belonging to the same class. Theories are not good at describing things in their completeness, or in their unique complexity. They operate within a metaphor that places the essence inside, in the depth of things, in the sphere which is invisible to the non-theoretical cognition (to Plato's *doxa*) that is satisfied with the apparent. Theoretical cognition aims at seeing through phenomena (appearances) to that which is thought to be more stable, persistent, and universal than the surface. However, with the very same gesture, like in an X-ray image, it makes the surface (the appearance) invisible. If we look at theories as discourses, these "theoretically invisible" particularities must be taken into account. A case analyzed in Chapter 4 presents this issue in a more systematic, historically specific way.

Yet another aspect of theoretical invisibility can relate to the source of light, to light at its utmost intensity. To refer to Plato's philosopher, his first experience after leaving the cave is that of blindness; he is dazzled by the brightness of ideas, and it takes time for him to realize that he can see them in their full light. This metaphor is perhaps more difficult to be turned into an analytical tool. It could suggest that when analyzing theories, one should pay attention to elements that illuminate their structures: to be more precise, to the concepts (if they are concepts) that make it possible to define other concepts. "If they are concepts" means here that such illuminating elements may themselves be impossible to define within the language of the theory; therefore, they may be "not conceptual enough" to become its normal elements. In formal languages, this could pertain to the status of axioms, of concepts that cannot be defined within a given language and are used to define its other concepts. In other words, if a concept is positioned as the foundation, or as the conclusion of a conceptual hierarchy, it is there "alone" – we cannot identify a class of concepts to which it belongs and we cannot, therefore, point to its *differentia specifica*. The classical definition demands that we point to the general (e.g., the human is *an animal*) and then to the specific (the human is a *rational* animal), and such a definition will not be possible if we try to define that which is the foundation of all other concepts in a given language. In less formalized languages, which are typical of the social sciences and the humanities, such central positions will be taken by rhetorical figures, first of all by metaphors. Metaphors are both the keystones which help to connect the elements of theory into viable structures and the openings taking us beyond the content of particular theoretical statements.[5]

The last instance of invisibility to identify here is the locus of the gaze – the place or position from which observation is made. The classic example of this kind of invisibility, which was mentioned previously, is the tower of the Panopticon. As Gilles Deleuze says, in Foucault the Panopticon is presented as a "luminous form that bathes the peripheral cells in light but leaves the central tower opaque, distributing prisoners who are seen but are not able to see, and the observer who sees everything without being seen. As statements are inseparable from systems, so visibilities are inseparable from machines" (Deleuze 1999, pp. 49–50).

Once again, I read *theoria* as the order of seeing. If we investigate educational theories as machines of visibility, the distribution of visibility means the selection of elements which are connectible and can build argumentative structures, and of those which have to remain opaque (for all, or for specific recipients of theoretical texts), or are simply excluded from the content. However, the issue of visibility and invisibility proves not only to be constitutive of the structure of theory: it is literally present as an important element of the content of educational theories. My Foucauldian/Rancièrean assumption is that wherever we encounter the instances of invisibility, we should be attentive to the operation of power, and, conversely, whenever theories speak about power, one should search for invisibility. In general, the construction of visibility and invisibility is an ontological thing; it is an act of construing totalities, of delimiting, through exclusion, their borders,[6] and, as such, it is ultimately a political issue. The case of The Panopticon is but an example here. Rancière's theory (2011), which defines politics as particular aesthetics that organize the distribution of the sensible, provides for broad applications of this idea. In other words, if we look at the suggested link between power and (in)visibility from the perspective of the political, to work effectively, the operation of modern technologies of power must be deeply inscribed into everyday practices so that they become naturalized and their work unnoticed. Gilles Deleuze (2006) says that the idea of invisibility of power is originally Nietzschean. According to Nietzsche, as conscious subjects, we are structured by *reactions* to the forces that are *active*. This means that, for our consciousness, what is active is beyond sight. Active forces conquer and suppress other forces. Those dominated become reactive to domination, and only as such can they be recognized consciously. As Deleuze notes, the problem pertains not only to subjective consciousness, but also to the construction of science.

> Consciousness merely expresses the relation of certain reactive forces to the active forces that dominate them. . . . What happens is that science follows the paths of consciousness, relying entirely on *other* reactive forces; the organism is always seen from its petty side, from the side of its reactions. . . . The true science is that of activity, but the science of activity is also the science of what is necessarily unconscious. The idea that science must follow consciousness in the footsteps of consciousness, in the same direction, is absurd. We can sense morality in that idea. In fact there can only be science where there is no consciousness, where there can be no consciousness.
>
> (Deleuze 2006, pp. 41–42)

Let us note, however, that, in the case of political power, this active and invisible force is a social construction itself. Its invisibility is, then, also socially constructed – and this is where I am looking for possible political uses of educational theory. What I am trying to say is that at least some varieties of the theoretical discourse of education can be investigated as such hiding and blinding instances, as structures that remove the operation of active social forces from the eyes of the public. Other connections between educational theories and modern politics, especially in their ontological dimensions, are embedded in more detailed analyses of particular theories and they cannot be announced in this introduction.

Apart from analyzing education theories as "visibility/invisibility machines," I read them as discursive constructions saturated with rhetorical devices. In more traditional approaches to theory, the presence of such devices is condemned as compromising the need for conceptual clarity, and, consequently, the chances of theory to be verified or falsified in empirical tests, which are possible when concepts to be operationalized are clearly distinguished from other concepts. However, theories of education are partially implicated in the construction of human and social identities, which stems from their theological and religious origins (Osterwalder 2012; Tröhler 2014; Tröhler, Popkewitz and Labaree 2011). According to Laclau (2005), the construction of political identity is impossible by purely conceptual, or logical means; it must resort to the figurative use of language. Moreover, Laclau's theory borrows some of its founding ideas from Jacques Lacan, which extends this necessity of rhetorics into the analyses of individual identities as well. This possibility of theorizing the political and the individual in one theoretical model is why I find Laclau's theory so promising in its applications to educational analyses (cf. Szkudlarek 2007; 2011; 2013; 2014). What it means in terms of this project is that the conceptual, explanatory structure of theories should be read together with their rhetorical dimensions – with their tropologies and rhetorical (persuasive, legitimizing, etc.) strategies and tactics. The analyses presented here are attentive to such rhetorical dimensions, and their aim is, first of all, to investigate how theories of education are implicated in the construction of not only individual subjectivities, but also, and foremost, of political identities, or totalities; what figures they employ, and how they utilize them in their attempts at creating given singularities, given objects that can be endowed with agency and force.

The theoretical assumptions, questions, and suppositions I am listing here guide my analyses in their initial stages, while actual interpretations follow the conceptual/rhetorical complexes specific to given theories rather than those that could be deduced as guiding hypotheses from the theoretical background hinted in this chapter. In other words, the rhetorical content of the theories I analyze proves to be richer than the themes of the invisibility of force and the rhetorical construction of totality suggest, and than the theories mentioned in this introduction can predict.

One can note that the issues of singularity, exclusion, and force connect to the themes of invisibility and totality. This foretells that their separateness will not be maintained throughout the course of analyses in the following chapters;

the understanding of *theoria* as the organization of visibility, with its political connotations elaborated by Nietzsche, Foucault, Deleuze, and Rancière, and the figurative aspect of discourse capable of creating identities, operate, in fact, as one and the same field in which the connections between education and politics are traced and interpreted. It is only in the last, concluding chapter that I return to their analytical differentiation, and I try to list some of the diverse tropes and strategies identified in educational theories around these guiding themes.

My investigation is based on just four historically and pedagogically diversified cases of educational theory. This means that the scope of the analyses presented henceforth is limited and that it does not exhaust "the question of educational theory" in general. I speak of Jean-Jacques Rousseau, of Johann Friedrich Herbart, of a Polish theory (and political discourse) of educating society as it was developed between the 1920s and the 1980s, and of the contemporary discourse of education in the knowledge-based society. Not all these complexes of educational ideas are, thus, theories in a narrowly scientific sense. Rousseau's political and educational philosophy probably does not meet the contemporary criteria of identifying a complex of ideas as a theory. A similar concern can be expressed as to the discourse of the knowledge-based society, which includes theoretical elements, but it operates, most of all, as a political doctrine. In the case of the Polish conception of educating society, we also encounter the combination of an academic theory (dating back to 1927) and a collection of later ideological and political textual practices. It seems, in general, that contemporary education is not informed by theories *sensu stricto*, not even in Continental Europe, where such traditions, or perhaps merely such an expectation, exist. I am, therefore, using the term "theory" in a broad sense, borrowing its meaning from the original *theoria* – as a complex of ideas which organize ways of seeing.

The order of analyses is chronological, but the following chapters do not form a historical text. Their analysis creates something like an insular structure, where particular historical conceptions illustrate various ways of articulating education and the political. What connects these islands is, undoubtedly, that they all operate within the horizon of modernity, and their historical diversity illustrates fragments of the rich heritage of modern ideas coined to reconstruct the always problematic relations between individual human beings and their states, or societies, as political agencies. Second, all these pedagogical ideas employ diverse rhetorical devices and strategies in order to claim their educational specificity, i.e., to distance themselves from other theoretical discourses and to build their singularity. To some extent, all these theories perform a dual gesture of disconnecting the individual from the political (first of all by identifying themselves as pedagogical) and of re-connecting them on their own terms. After all, they are all *modern* theories of education, and the reconstruction of the relation between the individual and the political is one of the main problems that modern societies continue to struggle with, which is a simple consequence of the invention of the individual human subject at the birth of modernity.

None of these analyses is complete in terms of them being congruent with the intentions of their founders or of their pedagogical richness and theoretical complexity. They are performed with the aim of identifying specific ways of linking the pedagogical and the political, but not with that of being complete historical or pedagogical reconstructions. As I have already declared in this chapter, the direction of these analyses is largely influenced by the work of Foucault, Laclau, and Rancière. Foucault is a classic of educational studies of the last decades, and, apart from some reminders provided in this chapter and scattered references in the following ones, I do not reconstruct or discuss his works in detail. The situation is different with Laclau's theory. Its educational implications are still not fully recognized, and his understanding of rhetoric and its role in the process of forming political identities is invaluable. At the same time, his theory needs to be fine-tuned for the needs of educational analyses. For these reasons, I devote Chapter 6 to discuss Laclau's ideas, simultaneously using them to interpret some of the findings throughout the book. Readers who are not familiar with Laclau's theory might consider reading Chapter 6, particularly the first section, before turning to the analysis of the four instances of educational theory presented in the following chapters. In the last chapter, I discuss the overall results of the analyses while focusing on the elements in educational theories which permit suggesting a meta-theoretical account on the role of rhetorics in theorizing education, and, specifically, on their role in the construction of visibility/invisibility and of singularities (identities, totalities) at the intersection of the pedagogical and the political, as the fundamental question of social ontology. At that stage, I discuss my findings in relation to the work of Jacques Rancière and of those thinkers who apply his ideas to revitalize the contemporary philosophy and theory of education.

The scope of analyses undertaken in this book cannot be satisfactory, either in historical terms (did it not all start with Plato?) or in pedagogical ones (why not analyze Dewey or critical pedagogy?). I have no doubts that such analyses should be taken up, and I am fully aware that the literature on the connections between education and politics is monumental. I do not review this literature here; nor do I discuss important, classic works (like Dewey or critical pedagogy) which address this theme. My choice of theories is guided by the intention to elicit as diverse a repertoire as possible of rhetorical tropes and educational *topoi*, applicable in the ontological construction of modern society, from a relatively minimal repertoire of theoretical conceptions. The sample is thus composed of just four cases that are diversified along three axes. First, I want to test the connections between the pedagogical and the political in somewhat contrasting pedagogical theories – hence, the choice of Rousseau, with his child-centered, naturalistic, "emotional" approach, on the one hand, and of Herbart, with his intellectualism, rigor, and teacher-centered pedagogy on the other. Second, I want to contrast the conceptions created in diverse political systems. Hence, on the one hand, I discuss the case of socialist pedagogy (the conception of educating society), on the one hand, and the neoliberal one (education in the knowledge-based society), on the other. Third, each of these conceptions represents a different century in the history of modernity (from the eighteenth to the twenty-first). My hope is that the span of the cases analyzed in a similar theoretical and methodological framework will result in a rich collection of tropologies and rhetorical strategies responsible for the connections between education and politics, and that the results will enhance our understanding of how educational theories – with all their weakness, marginality, and conceptual ambiguity – can be constitutive elements of political ontologies. I can only hope that this direction of reading theories of education will be continued, and that the preliminary findings proposed in this book are confronted with more detailed, broader, and, perhaps, more accurate research.

How, then, is the politics of theory in education understood in this book? The final answer will be suggested in the concluding chapter. What I can say now is that I am searching for the *ways of construing* theories of education, including their rhetorics, rather than their specific conceptual claims alone, that can be identified as contributing to the construction of political identities.

Notes

1   I have offered a preliminary, concise outline of this perspective in a previous publication (Szkudlarek 2014), which I recommend as an overview of the issues I address in this book.

2   Laclau and Mouffe (1985) use the notion of hegemony in the meaning proposed by Antonio Gramsci. However, in the last version of this theory, Laclau (2005; 2014) maintains that the operation of hegemony is structurally identical to the operation of catachresis in classical rhetoric, and to the function of *objet petit a* in the Lacanian psychoanalysis. See Chapter 6 for a more detailed presentation of Laclau's theory.

3   The following excerpt is based on my previously published text (Szkudlarek 2014).

4   This was the case in Germany and, through this inspiration, in Continental Europe. Such development did not take place in England or the USA, where problems of education were theorized within other disciplinary fields, like medicine, philosophy, child psychology, or sociology. See Biesta G., 2011.

5   This assumption relates to deconstruction and to such theories in which rhetorics are given ontological status. A perfect example could be the analysis of the notion of *khora* (place) in Plato by Jacques Derrida, where the concept keeps elapsing all subsequent attempts at explanation and eventually gains a mystical status of that which makes other concepts possible, while remaining outside conceptualization itself. There is a moment in the text where Derrida gives this figurative agency a quasi-personal, or godly, status asking: *Who are you, khora?* (Derrida 1995, p. 111). In Ernesto Laclau's theory, the hegemonic function in the process of identity construction (which he understands as a semiotic process) is played by empty signifiers, which are catachreses in rhetorical terms. Both Derrida and Laclau were inspired by Lacan and the psychoanalytical idea of emptiness in the center of subjectivity.

6   It is easy to note that a totality which needs exclusion in order to define its borders is not a totality. This is precisely how Laclau understands political totalities, or identities; they are always "failed" totalities. See Laclau, 2005, and Chapter 6 for more details.

References

BAKER, B. (2001). (Ap)pointing the Canon. Rousseau's Emile, Visions of the State, and Education. *Educational Theory*, 51 (Winter), pp. 1–43.

BALL, S. (ed.) (1990). *Foucault and Education: Disciplines and Knowledge.* London: Routledge.

BAUDRILLARD, J. (1995). Radical Thought. [Online]. *Ctheory.* Available from: www.ctheory.net/articles.aspx?id=67. [Accessed: 14th February 14, 2016].

BENTHAM, J. (1791). *Panopticon; or, the Inspection – House: Containing The Idea of a New Principles of Construction Applicable to any Sort of Establishment, in which Persons of any Description are to be Kept under Inspection: And in particular to Prisons, Houses of Industry, Work – Houses, Poor – Houses, Manufactories, Mad – Houses, Lazarettos, Hospitals, and Schools.* Dublin and London: T. Payne.

BIESTA, G. (2011). Disciplines and Theory in the Academic Study of Education: A Comparative Analysis of the Anglo-Saxon and Continental Construction of the Field. *Pedagogy, Culture and Society*, 19, pp. 175–192.

BIESTA, G., ALLAN, J. and EDWARDS, R. (2014). Introduction: The Theory Question in Education and the Education Question in Theory. In BIESTA, G., ALLAN, J. and EDWARDS, R. (eds.) *Making a Difference in Theory. The Theory Question in Education and the Education Question in Theory.* London: Routledge.

DELEUZE, G. (1999). *Foucault.* New York: Continuum.

DELEUZE, G. (2006). *Nietzsche and Philosophy.* New York: Columbia University Press.

DERRIDA, J. (1995). *On the Name.* Stanford: Stanford University Press.

DERRIDA, J. (1997). *Of Grammatology.* Baltimore: Johns Hopkins University Press.

FOUCAULT, M. (1980). *Power/Knowledge. Selected Interviews and other Writings 1972–1977.* New York: Pantheon Books.

FOUCAULT, M. (ed.) (1982). *I, Pierre Rivière, Having Slaughtered My Mother, My Sister, and My Brother . . . : A Case of Parricide in the 19th Century.* Lincoln: University of Nebraska Press.

FOUCAULT, M. (1995). *Discipline and Punish: The Birth of the Prison.* New York: Vintage Books

HABERMAS, J. (1972). *Knowledge and Human Interests.* Boston: Beacon Press.

HABERMAS, J. (1984). *Theory of Communicative Action Volume One: Reason and the Rationalization of Society.* Boston: Beacon Press.

HERBART, J.F. (1908). *The Science of Education. Its General Principles Deduced from Its Aim, and the Aesthetic Revelation of the World.* Cambridge, Boston: D.C. Heath & Co., Publishers.

KANT, I. (1993). *Grounding for the Metaphysics of Morals.* Indianapolis, Cambridge: Hackett Publishing Company.

LACLAU, E. (2005). *On Populist Reason.* London: Verso.

LACLAU, E. (2014). *The Rhetorical Foundations of Society.* London: Verso.

LACLAU, E. and MOUFFE, Ch. (1985). *Hegemony and Socialist Strategy. Towards a Radical Democratic Politics.* London: Verso.

MARSHALL, J.D. (1996). *Michel Foucault: Personal Autonomy and Education.* Dordrecht, Boston and London: Kluwer.

MOUFFE, Ch. (2005). *The Return of the Political.* London: Verso.

OSTERWALDER, F. (2012). The Modern Religious Language of Education: Rousseau's Emile. *Studies in Philosophy and Education*, 31, pp. 432–447.

POPKEWITZ, T. (2014). The Empirical and Political 'Fact' of Theory in the Age of Knowledge Capitalism. In BIESTA, G., ALLAN, J. and EDWARDS, R. (eds.) *Making a Difference in Theory. The Theory Question in Education and the Education Question in Theory*. London: Routledge.

RANCIÈRE, J. (2011). *The Politics of Aesthetics. The Distribution of the Sensible*. London: Continuum International Publishing Group.

SCHMITT, C. (1996). *The Concept of the Political*. Chicago: Chicago University Press.

SZKUDLAREK. T. (1995). Pedagogizm i pedagogika. In HEJNICKA-BEZWIŃSKA, T. (ed.) *Racjonalność pedagogiki*. Bydgoszcz: Wyższa Szkoła Pedagogiczna.

SZKUDLAREK, T. (2003). Educational Theory, Displacement, and Hegemony. *International Journal of Applied Semiotics*, 4 (2), pp. 109–130.

SZKUDLAREK, T. (2007). Empty Signifiers, Politics and Education. *Studies in Philosophy and Education*, 26 (3), pp. 237–252.

SZKUDLAREK, T. (2011). Semiotics of Identity. Education and Politics. *Studies in Philosophy and Education*, 30 (2), pp. 113–125.

SZKUDLAREK, T. (2013). Identity and Normativity: Politics and Education. In SZKUDLAREK, T. (ed.) *Education and the Political. New Theoretical Articulations*. Rotterdam, Boston and Taipei: Sense Publishers.

SZKUDLAREK, T. (2014). The Excess of Theory. On the Functions of Educational Theory in Apparent Reality. In BIESTA, G., ALLAN, J. and EDWARDS, R. (eds.) *Making a Difference in Theory. The Theory Question in Education and the Education Question in Theory*. London: Routledge.

TRÖHLER, D. (2014). Between Universally Claimed Theory and a Common Understanding: Theorhertical Knowledge in Education. In BIESTA, G., ALLAN, J. and EDWARDS, R. (eds.) *Making a Difference in Theory. The Theory Question in Education and the Education Question in Theory*. London and New York: Routledge.

TRÖHLER, D., POPKEWITZ, T.S. and LABAREE, D.F. (eds.) (2011). *Schooling and the Making of Citizens in the Long Nineteenth Century. Comparative visions*. New York and London: Routledge.

ŽIŽEK, S. (1992). *Looking Awry: An Introduction to Jacques Lacan Through Popular Culture*. Cambridge, MA: MIT Press.

Chapter 2

Education, society, and the nation. "I have decided to be what you made me"

Rousseau

Jean-Jacques Rousseau's conception of education is one of the most influential in the history of modern Europe, and it still inspires numerous and diverse interpretations: not only because of its richness, but also because of its almost proverbial ambiguity and its often paradoxical rhetoric.

In this chapter, I am not trying to reconstruct the body of Rousseau's work in its whole complexity. Rather, it is a selective analysis through which I aim to identify topics and tropes which allow for systematic and complex transitions between education and politics. My intention, as I have mentioned in the previous chapter, is to look at Rousseau's ontology by reconstructing the conceptual structure of his work together with its rhetorical devices. I focus, first of all, on *Emile, or Education* (Rousseau 1921), trying to reconstruct the connections between the conceptions of the child, nature, and divinity as the scaffolding for the analysis of the concept of education. In this triangle, the ambiguity of nature plays a pivotal role. I also refer to Rousseau's political works, including a rarely discussed text on the political system of Poland, where the same triadic structure is supplemented with the concept of nation and where the issue of civic education – apparently different from that exposed in *Emile* – is discussed. Within this structure, I am analyzing the transitions between the registers of the pedagogical and the political.

Nature, education, and invisibility

An often discussed feature of Rousseau's rhetoric is his inclination to paradox. As Bronisław Baczko (1966) notes, paradoxes are taken by Rousseau "seriously," as reflecting real antagonisms and impossibilities – a topos that will be "elevated to the dignity of theory" in the work of Laclau. The opening paragraphs of *Emile* expose this paradoxical rhetoric very well:

> God makes all things good; man[1] meddles with them and they become evil. He forces one soil to yield the products of another, one tree to bear another's fruit. He confuses and confounds time, place, and natural conditions. . . . He destroys and defaces all things; he loves all that is

deformed and monstrous; he will have nothing as nature made it, not even man himself...Yet things would be worse without...education....Under existing conditions a man left to himself from birth would be more of a monster than the rest.... She would be like a sapling chance sown in the midst of the highway, bent hither and thither and soon crushed by the passers-by .... Plants are fashioned by cultivation, man by education. We are born weak, we need strength; helpless, we need aid; foolish, we need reason. All that we lack at birth, all that we need when we come to man's estate, is the gift of education.

(Rousseau 1921, pp. 5–6)

The lamentation of the destruction of nature does not sound like an introduction to praise for education, inevitably involved in the "meddling" with human nature; and yet education – as in the reference to the sapling – is presented as capable of saving the natural from destructive civilization. This single excerpt creates the structure of oppositions and ambiguities which invite the conception of negative pedagogy proposed by Rousseau, as Jean Starobinski says (1971), foretelling the Hegelian structure of the negation of negation.

As many researchers suggest, nature is the most ambiguous concept of Rousseau's philosophy (cf. Baczko 1966; Baker 2001b). Nature, as the creation of God, is "good" but "imperfect": it is incomplete, marked by lack and absence, and vulnerable to human destruction. It is weak and has to be supplemented by education. At the same time, in contrast to the idea of saving nature by education, Rousseau is perfectly aware that we are on the way of no return. He uses the concept of "natural man," but he makes it clear that it is an idealized state of the beginnings of humanity that, if it had ever existed, cannot be transplanted to the contemporary. Once we have decided to divide the Earth into individual properties (*The Social Contract*), the irreversible process of supplementing nature, including our own, with human creations, has begun. We may question the moral value of such substitutions, but we are their products ourselves.

The idea that it is nature rather than civilization that provides a proper environment for the growing child (Rousseau advocates removing children from town life and educating them in the country) is not, therefore, the one of return. Education has to take a circular path: it has to evade, or detour the evils of civilization, and speak to that which is – potentially, if we manage to reveal it – natural in us. It has to follow from the present state of oblivion, to the *implied* naturalness, and from there it can aim at the future. With all the concern with the lost paradise of natural men, Rousseau's pedagogy – by virtue of bypassing the present – has a potential to be revolutionary.[2]

Natural education in Rousseau is not, thus, about letting the child experience nature "as it is": naturalness is staged and controlled. Emile is accompanied and supervised by his tutor who should administer the "right" experiences to the child. However, the appeals to control the experience of the child are accompanied by constant reminders that teachers must be discreet and silent. Rousseau advocates *negative pedagogy* in the early period of a child's development, which means the prevention of evil rather than the construction of the good (the good is already there – the child is "good by nature"). Secondly, the inaction of the teacher is more valuable than action:

> Zealous teachers, be simple, discrete, and reticent. Be in no hurry to act unless to prevent the actions of others. . . . [R]eject, if it may be, a good lesson for fear of giving a bad one. Beware of playing the tempter in this world, which nature intended as an earthly paradise for men, and do not attempt to give the innocent child the knowledge of good and evil.
>
> (Rousseau 1921, p. 60)

Rousseau's rhetoric operates within the Biblical myth here. It was the failure of Adam and Eve to resist the temptation to gain "knowledge of good and evil" that led God to expel them from Eden. The paragraph reads as if Rousseau wants to interrupt the repetition of the history of the Fall of Man in every human life, to keep the child in a semblance of Eden and, thus, to break the cycle of the reproduction of evil. The innocent purity of the child, shielded from premature experience and slowed down in learning the unnecessary, helps to safeguard the unrestricted influence of the teacher in further steps of education; it prevents not only the impact of the corrupt world, but the resistance of the child as well. "Without prejudice and without habits, there would be nothing in him to counteract the effects of your labours. In your hands he would soon become the wisest of men; by doing nothing to begin with, you would end with a prodigy of education" (1921, pp. 57–58). The tutor, discouraged from frequent direct interventions, operates mainly by controlling the learning environment, of which he himself is a part.

> Remember you must be a man yourself before you try to train a man; you yourself must set the pattern he shall copy. While the child is still unconscious there is time to prepare his surroundings, so that nothing shall strike his eye but what is fit for his sight. Gain the respect of every one, begin to win their hearts, so that they may try to please you. You will not be master of the child if you cannot control every one about him; and this authority will never suffice unless it rests upon respect for your goodness.
>
> (1921, p. 59)

It is the arrangement of physical and social space that inspires the child to explore reality and prevents him from premature or improper experience. A very important thing is that the work of the teacher as the author of such an arrangement, including the arrangements of the personal features he had acquired while preparing himself for the role, are hidden from the sight of the child. The figure of the teacher is thus split along the line of visibility: being physically and visibly present as a part of the educating environment of the child, he stays invisible as the author of this environment and of himself as the educating persona.

With this observation we have thus exposed the intriguing figure of *the invisibility of the educating agent* as one of the premises on which the modern idea of education was built. The instance of invisibility, as that of significant absence, is more than a technical invention here. In the following section, I propose to interpret it in two perspectives. First is a mythical one composed of two interconnected and somewhat colliding figures of divinity. Second is the Nietzschean idea of the invisibility of active force, which is most widely known through the Foucauldian concept of the asymmetry of seeing and the notion of dispersed disciplinary control.

Invisibility and divinity

The notion of natural environment as suitable for the early development of the child is construed by Rousseau in accordance with the Biblical vision of Eden. Emile is innocent, he lives close to nature, and he should be prevented from learning the knowledge of good and evil (as in *Genesis* 3:5). It is worth noting that such religious connotation is by no means specific to Rousseau's pedagogy: it was fundamental for the emergence of the lay discourse of education in modern Europe. Its structure was built on the topics of religious debates of the time, especially within Protestant denominations (Osterwalder 2012; Tröhler 2014; Tröhler, Popkewitz, and Labaree 2011). As Fritz Osterwalder notes, Rousseau's ideas of education presented in *Emile* (unlike those expressed in his accounts on republican education, as in *The Social Contract*) were strongly influenced by the Piety movement in the Protestant church and the Jansenist movement in the Catholic one, both referring to the Augustinian tradition. Osterwalder points to the role that the Jansenist school of the Cistercian abbey in Port-Royal played in Rousseau's thought. The role of the tutor in guiding the pupil's transformation in isolation from the corrupt world, the stress on solitude and the low pace of learning, the treatment of child's innocence as holy, or such theoretical concepts as *amour propre* and *amour de soi* find their predecessors in the practice and the writings associated with these movements. As Osterwalder notes, Rousseau's account on the education of Emile "follows the theological – pedagogical concept of the piety movement almost to the letter" (p. 443). Moreover, Rousseau follows the style of religious writing as well: his "rhetoric layout . . . follows the theological tradition. The text does not just talk about education; instead, the writer addresses the reader directly and educates him thus to become an educator himself" (p. 444). Quoting Baczko, Osterwalder notes that Rouessau's treatises assume the function of a new gospel: teachers and legislators (in *The Social Contract*) are charged with "superhuman tasks"; they are projected as "divine figures" (p. 444).

The lines of continuity of religious discourse in Rousseau are strikingly strong. However, there is a splitting line as well, and it is a scandalous one.

Rousseau challenges the Christian dogma of the original sin and claims that the child is *born* as innocent, rather than being made so by the act of christening. The line of the continuation of Christian theological language is broken in the very beginning of the educational trajectory: at the moment of birth of the child. It is there that the goodness of the child is constituted, and it is from that point that it needs to be protected against the bad world. In consequence, salvation needs no church – the only gospel, as we read in *Profession of Faith of the Savoyard Vicar*, is the "book of nature." Following the religious mission, education displaces and replaces it in the work of transforming the soul on the way to salvation.

The similarity of Rousseau's vision of natural education to the figure of Eden is not accidental, then, and the invisibility of the teacher can be read through this metaphor. Apart from the idea of an invisible God who speaks through His creations, and occasionally through prophets and revelations, one can find another instance of invisibility in Genesis. After having violated the prohibition of eating the fruit of knowledge of good and evil, Adam and Eve hide from the gaze of God among the trees of the garden. It seems that Rousseau plays with both these tropes, creating a mythico-theoretical structure composed of pedagogical and theological narratives on the creation of the human. Following the first of these metaphors, one may say that the teacher, as the *author of things*, as the one who created the environment of learning for his pupil, hides himself before human eyes behind his creation. The nature of the child, revealed through careful and self-restricted education, will speak for the teacher. This interpretation can be illustrated by numerous excerpts of Rousseau's text, for instance by his account on the role of the tutor in arranging the marriage between Emile and Sophy.

> Instead of providing a wife for Emile in childhood, I have waited till I knew what would suit him. It is not for me to decide, but for nature; my task is to discover the choice she has made. . . . Do not suppose, however, that I have delayed to find a wife for Emile till I sent him in search of her. This search is only a pretext for acquainting him with women, so that he may perceive the value of a suitable wife. Sophy was discovered long since; Emile may even have seen her already, but he will not recognise her till the time is come.
>
> (Rousseau 1921, p. 331)

Similar to a previously quoted excerpt, where Rousseau advocates that the teacher change the surroundings of Emile *before* he is conscious, the above paragraph speaks of a certain temporal encroaching, of *determining the future of the child by controlling his past*, of creating his world before the time of his arrival. The precautions taken before the child enters the scene of experience allow the teacher to almost rest in inaction when the time of experience comes; they create the conditions allowing for his pedagogy to be negative and, by leaving the present to apparently natural experiences, make it invisible to the child. In the child's presence, the teacher has only to control the purity of the scene; to prevent it from being intruded upon by things from other temporal settings (premature experiences) or strangers acting in line with uncontrolled scripts. The time for such alien encounters, *travel* time – in the paragraph about marriage represented by "acquainting with women" – comes later, in a similarly prescribed way. Such temporal encroachment on the part of the teacher, turning the course of lived experience into a prescribed curriculum, becomes visible to Emile only *a posteriori*, in a retrospective gesture of synthesis, when the pupil is capable of seeing his teacher through the memories of his experience. It leaves Emile with only one option on his way to personhood: "What decision have I come to? I have decided to be what you made me" (Rousseau 1921, p. 390). Indeed, the temporal dimension of Rousseau's pedagogy foretells the Hegelian dialectic of identity.

As I have mentioned before, another mythical interpretation of the invisibility of the teacher may follow the metaphor of Adam and Eve hiding from the sight of God. Can one say that Emile's teacher keeps himself invisible in a similar way? Such a possibility invites two questions. First, whose gaze does he hide from? Second, what might the tutor feel guilty or ashamed of, or what kind of guilt is implied in the work of the teacher? Is it not only the teacher, but also the child who is placed in the position of God in *Emile*? Bernadette Baker finds such a godly trait in the writing about children as early as in John Locke, pointing to the transcendent character of the child in his works (Baker 2001a, p. 175). Apart from its mythical (Biblical) context, this interpretation may relate to the fact that in Rousseau's time, the idea of nature as connected to divinity was popular. In *Profession of Faith of a Savoyard Vicar*, Rousseau presents a theological argument based on the Newtonian definition of movement, whence he infers the notion of universal Will that is responsible for spontaneous movements and harmony in nature. This idea, as well as the observation that our morals ground in natural sentiments ("love for the good"), forms the basis for Rousseau's natural religion that needs no reference to theological speculation, explication, or condemnation; neither to miracles nor to revelations. "There is one book which is open to every one – the book of nature. In this good and great volume I learn to serve and adore its Author. There is no excuse for not reading this book; for it speaks to all in a language they can understand" (Rousseau 1921, p. 242).

If we follow the idea that the child remains close to that which is natural in man, Emile himself may be seen as part of this divine book of nature, and through him can the teacher "learn to serve and adore its Author." Accordingly, indecent human deeds (like those of "meddling" with the creation, manipulating it so that its nature is distorted, as in the opening paragraph of *Emile*), may be a reason for shame and can make one avoid the transparent eyes of the child through which the Author of nature is seen. Can one say that education, in its manipulative manner proposed by Rousseau, is a reason for shame? Can it make the teacher feel guilty? The education of Emile is based on deception. If nature speaks through the child, the child is thus God's gospel. It is not unthinkable, then, that the teacher's work better be hidden from the controlling, natural, and innocent gaze of the child, just as before the Exodus the first humans had to evade the eye of God. In other words, if God speaks through nature, and the child is the instance of nature in man, one who educates should fear the gaze of the child.

The hiding of the intent and the actions of Emile's teacher can thus be interpreted as following the duality of the child who is both natural (and thus, through metonymic connections, divine) and incomplete (and thus subject to supplementation). The godly teacher makes a human of the child, and blasphemously profanes the godly nature of the child. The human teacher fears the godly nature of the child, keeps silent about his own godly deeds, and presents himself as inactive. Education based on the myth of nature profanes nature as "the book of God" and reveals it at the same time.

Rousseau seeks theological justification for his claims, and to legitimize his projects of managing societies and human souls, he gives his naturalism a religious form. Thus positioned, education tends to erase its work; it "prefers" to remain silent and invisible. Its secure work depends on the art of manipulating the environment which allows the teacher to make her work invisible.

> [Let the child] always think he is master while you are really master. There is no subjection so complete as that which preserves the forms of freedom; it is thus that the will itself is taken captive. . . . No doubt he ought only to do what he wants, but he ought to want to do nothing but what you want him to do. He should never take a step you have not foreseen, nor utter a word you could not foretell.
>
> (Rousseau 1921, p. 80)

The child's nature is thus saved from the devastating influence of the spoiled society, and safe from direct intervention that teachers might irreverently commit. In the humble service of a nonexistent society, the teacher works against the existent one, gently taking the child a hostage of the utopian future.

The complex structure of links between nature, goodness, and divinity, with their supplement of education resorting to deception, presented rhetorically as control over temporality (slowing down the time of growth, encroachment into the past to control the future) and over the spatiality of the child (moving to the country, arranging every detail of the space of experience) work toward the naturalization of education. In fact, from the position of the child, education is erased; it is replaced by a simulation of free will and natural experience. The cultural construction of the conditions and the stimuli of that experience are made invisible. In short, the *culture of nature* (the cultural construction employing nature for social and political goals) is substituted for the *nature of culture*: for its formative, cultivating, ultimately pedagogical work (Szkudlarek 2005).

Invisibility and emptiness in social control

The task of repairing the damage of civilization and building the republic can be completed only if the creation of new human beings takes indirect route, by creating proper institutional conditions. This is where the mythical figure of the invisible Author of education, who creates the world for the child to grow according to nature, meets the instances of surveillance and power/knowledge analyzed in Michel Foucault's (1995) work. We have thus arrived at the second perspective for interpreting *Emile*, not mythical, but socio-ontological. Education – in its mechanical, disciplinary, and panoptic aspects related to the environmental design of its business – is one of crucial practices responsible for the construction of modernity.

There is a Nietzschean idea, further developed by Gilles Deleuze and Michel Foucault, that power is invisible. According to Nietzsche, we are *reactive* to force, and it is our reactions that inform us of its existence (Deleuze 2002). The writing of Rousseau, in this respect, operates on two levels. On the one hand, it postulates and thus reveals the operation of power by advocating that teachers purposefully construct a milieu in which the child will learn. On the other, he advocates that such arrangements are made invisible to the child. At the same time, Rousseau's rhetoric legitimizes this indirect and invisible form of control. Naming his pedagogy negative, and presenting it as preventive rather than formative, overshadows the undoubtedly positive aspect of Rousseau's education, which dwells in the management of the surroundings prepared for the child.

The hiding of such environmental control of experience, expressed in postulational language as valuable (natural, benign, effective, permissive) is the main instrument of making power invisible in Rousseau. It is made rhetorically possible owing to the way Rousseau uses the concept of nature. Bronisław Baczko (1964, p. 46) says that "any attempt at defining nature in Rousseau's text is futile," and Bernadette Baker identifies its "at least six, sometimes overlapping meanings":

> Nature appears as an original state (e.g., *First* and *Second Discourse*), as untamed animal appetites without religious or moral reasonings (e.g., *Second Discourse*), as matter and force (e.g., *Emile*), as uniform laws of motion (*Emile*), as that which is not made by humans (e.g. *First Discourse*), and as those potentials or dispositions that are revealed a posteriori by institutions Man founds (e.g., *The Social Contract*).
>
> (Baker 2001a, p. 233)

Although the modern notion of the child is inscribed in all these meanings, it is the last one that applies directly to the problem discussed here showing the ambiguity of the origins and their supplementation, or, more precisely, pointing to the nature of the child becoming visible *providing that we educate him according to his nature*. As Peter Trifonas (2000, p. 250) says, in Rousseau "nature works twice." Derrida (1997) relates this circular work of nature to the notion of supplement in Rousseau. In Rousseau's reflections on writing, civil society, education, or masturbation, the secondary (like writing or masturbation) supplements the natural (like speech or love). Derrida reads Rousseau's notion of supplement as substitution, an excess, scandal, something ambivalent, but at the same time as the condition of seeing that which is supplemented. In Rousseau, we know what is natural when our action, based on that which we *imply* as such, produces results which we accept *as* natural. "Immediacy is derived," says Derrida (1997, p. 157). We cannot have access to nature in the human. It has to be implied, and only as such may it work as the foundation for the work of education

The complexity of nature in Rousseau is an outcome of the rhetorical strategy of his writing as much as it is its condition. Vagueness, or emptiness, is a condition, a function, and a product of importance. Its role can be explained in light of Laclau's theory (2005; 2014). The conflicting tasks Rousseau undertakes (like educating "within and against civil society," Baker 2001b, p. 221) can be addressed only where there is the notion that provides space for such efforts, and that notion must be vague, not only because it cannot be defined by what it tries to give ground for, but also for the very sake of the feasibility of the political project. According to Laclau (see Chapter 6), social structures can be constructed only in relation to empty signifiers, and only such figures are capable of articulating the incommensurable demands of which Rousseau speaks when he resorts to his paradoxes. In other words, if nature works as the instance that links past and future, education and politics, collectivity and individuality, it cannot be defined in a logical manner; nor can it work as a concept. Not only does the opaqueness of nature help to construe the argument that cannot be reduced to that for or against civil society, but it gives space for such tension being articulated at all. The installation of nature as the central concept of Rousseau's philosophy, and – in the context of such centrality – the somewhat "disappointing" vagueness of this concept, is not accidental, even though it invites a circular, proto-Hegelian logic. Kevin Inston (2010) notes that the construction of the human as natural, which is performed by subtracting, or stripping the human of all that can be identified as socially constructed, leads to the subsequent denouncement of modern society as alien to such naturalness, and eventually to the claim that *society has no natural foundations*. This statement has revolutionary consequences. Inston argues that Rousseau's work foretells the radical theory of democracy proposed by Laclau and Mouffe.

> The negativity of nature – its subtraction of any social content – emphasizes its radical difference from society. That negativity does not signify nothingness, but rather the negation of determinacy: society, without any final and total ground, can never be fully determined, remaining always available to reconfiguration. Rousseau criticizes previous philosophers for not looking

beyond the given in order to reactivate the political moment of social construction. While their theories of nature naturalized society, Rousseau's theory "de-naturalizes" it. Nature, despite its fictional quality, is necessary for understanding the present moment as a mere possibility rather than as an inexorable outcome.

(Inston 2010, p. 26)

The question which should be asked in this context is the following: what is the relation between *education* being construed as natural and the constructibility of society? What is the political meaning of education made invisible, naturalized, rendered negative? The first answer suggested thus far is that this relation is based on the instance of invisibility of social control. Rousseau's naturalism, the *culture of Nature* he creates, hides *the nature of culture*: it hides social control inscribed into cultural arrangements, texts, and meanings. This interpretation is indebted to Foucault's analyses of visibility as constitutive to modern power relations (Foucault 1995). At the same time, Foucault helps to see education as political (Hoskin 1990; Marshall 1996). Power cares, transmits knowledge, prevents deviation, examines, classifies, and allocates individuals in social space. All these verbs describe modern education as well. Rousseau's pedagogy postulates some of these techniques, but names them so that they present themselves as natural and negative, which actually means that they *de-present* themselves, that they make themselves invisible. Such a naturalization of education erases or makes invisible the work toward the political reconstruction of society.

How can we read, in this context, the political writings of Rousseau? There, too, the interplay between the natural and that which is made by man is in constant motion. Natural order is far better than an artificial one; natural and savage men have virtues that are extinct in civil societies. But we have to live in modern states. Therefore, we need to construe them "according to our nature" so that they do not enslave us, so that our natural goodness and liberty are maintained. As we read in *The Social Contract*:

> The problem is to find a form of association which will defend and protect with the whole common force the person and goods of each associate, and in which each, while uniting himself with all, may still obey himself alone, and remain as free as before. This is the fundamental problem of which the Social Contract provides the solution.
>
> (Rousseau 1923, p. 43)

This implies the mutual recognition of differences and the common recognition of general will: of the goodness of togetherness. The ambiguity of nature in this political construction helps to establish the horizon of universal freedom in which forms of togetherness are possible, and against which forms of government can be judged. The solutions proposed by Rousseau are, of course, complex and not easily reconcilable, especially when *The Social Contract* is read together with the more specific advice on the reform of the political system of Poland (Rousseau 1972).

The nation: Nature and estrangement

Considérations sur le gouvernement de Pologne et sur sa réformation projetée (The Government of Poland in the best known English translation; thereafter, referred to as *Considerations*)[3] was completed by Rousseau in 1772, when Poland was undergoing delayed political reforms aimed at strengthening the power of the state. The ineffective Polish democracy (where the *demos* was restricted to land owners) with kings appointed in free elections and their role reduced to executive power, made the country unable to stand the military pressure of its more powerful, authoritarian neighbors. The reforms initiated by King Stanisław August Poniatowski, supported by intellectuals inspired by French rationalism, met firm resistance from the nobility, which was threatened with the prospect of losing their almost unrestricted political power. Rousseau was invited to write his advice for alternative reforms by Count Michał Wielohorski, a representative of a powerful confederation opposing royal reforms.

Rousseau's text is usually read as a supplementary source in the analyses of *The Social Contract*. While some authors see the book as a context-specific implementation of *The Social Contract*, many point to discrepancies between the two texts and, first of all, to the overtones of conservatism in *Considerations* as opposed to some radicalism of *The Social Contract*. However, as Harvey Mansfield Jr. notes in the preface to the American edition of *Considerations*, the fundamental consistency between the two texts is their radical criticism of large nation-states as a form of political organization (Rousseau 1972). This critique was almost unnoticed by Rousseau's readers. Mansfield suggests that Rousseau must have been aware of how "unthinkable" this idea was and wanted to avoid public ridicule; at the same time, he strongly believed that the solution of the problem to which he devoted *The Social Contract* (which was "to find a form of association which will defend and protect . . . the person and goods of each associate," Rousseau 1923, p. 43) will be possible only in communities smaller than the dominant states of Europe. Meeting both of these concerns was possible only owing to Rousseau's rhetorical skill. "One of Rousseau's techniques for concealing something is that of making it simultaneously obvious and (for most readers) invisible," says Mansfield (xxix). That Rousseau could be frankly overt on this issue while writing about Poland is also a matter of rhetoric: of the opening declaration of distance to the country.

As a prelude to the blueprint for reform, the first pages of *Considerations* include the critique of the condition of the state.

> While reading the history of the government of Poland, it is hard to understand how a state so strangely constituted has been able to survive so long. A large body made up of a large number of dead members, and of

a small number of disunited members whose movements, being virtually independent of one another, are so far from being directed to a common end that they cancel each other out; a body which exerts itself greatly to accomplish nothing; which is capable of offering no sort of resistance to anyone who tries to encroach upon it; which falls into dissolution five or six times a century; which falls into paralysis whenever it tries to make any effort or to satisfy any need; and which, in spite of all this, lives and maintains its vigour: that, in my opinion, is one of the most singular spectacles ever to challenge the attention of a rational being.

(Rousseau 1972, p. 1)

This description is contrasted to remarks on other countries:

I see all the states of Europe rushing to their ruin. Monarchies, republics, all these nations for all their magnificent institutions, all these fine governments for all their prudent checks and balances, have grown decrepit and threaten soon to die; while Poland, a depopulated, devastated and oppressed region, defenceless against her aggressors and at the height of her misfortunes and anarchy, still shows all the fire of youth; she dares to ask for a government and for laws, as if she were newly born. She is in chains, and discusses the means of remaining free; she feels in herself the kind of force that the forces of tyranny cannot overcome.

(1972, pp. 1–2)

Today, no matter what people may say, there are no longer any Frenchmen, Germans, Spaniards, or even Englishmen; there are only Europeans. All have the same tastes, the same passions, the same manners, for no one has been shaped along national lines by peculiar institutions.

(1972, p. 5)

The *strangeness* of Poland is thus contrasted not to supposed normality of other countries, but to the mood of decay and the lack of national character elsewhere. Even though Poland is presented as impotent, chaotic, vulnerable, and lacking integrity, through the contrast to amorphousness rather than to strength it may at the same time be described as natural, young, vigorous, free, and sincere.

Why should Rousseau choose such juxtaposition? Apart from his general fascination with paradoxes pointing to real contradictions and ambivalence, the initial estrangement of Poland works as a tool for positioning Poland outside the dominant ways of understanding politics. Thus displaced, Poland may take the position of the undecidable from which the political in general is critically interrogated. In other words, while speaking of such a remote and bizarre place, Rousseau does not have to use abstract language in his critique of large nation-states as inclined to tyranny. On another, intrinsic level, estrangement puts Poland in a position that makes it possible for Rousseau to supplement the concept of the nation with two other meaningful categories: those of nature (Poland is close to the ancient "source" of nationhood) and childhood (she is young). Both *natio* and *natura* are derivatives of *natus* (born), which links nation with nature, and makes both concepts ready for metaphorical infantilization. Such supplementation is apparently at odds with *The Social Contract*, where the construction of society demands certain "denaturing" of men (I will return to this issue soon). Retrospectively, "nature" and "childhood" will work to naturalize the otherness of Poland constructed in the opening critique of the state. The following section will investigate these hypothetical connections in more detail.

Nations as children

The opening phrase of Book One of Rousseau's *The Social Contract* reads as follows: "I mean to inquire if, in the civil order, there can be any sure and legitimate rule of administration, men being taken as they are and laws as they might be" (Rousseau 1923, p. 34). "Men as they are" speaks to the notion of nature. To recall Baker's typology, (2001b, p. 233), it seems to mean men in their "original state," not "made" by other humans, but probably those in the present form of society as well. In spite of the somewhat foundational statement suggesting that we know what men "are," Inston (2010) notes that in *The Second Discourse* Rousseau was clear that the concept of nature can be made only by way of subtraction. Natural man arrives as, so to say, residuum, as that which cannot be explained as a product of social relations; "natural man" might have never existed. Following Inston, naturalness thus construed, on the way back toward the contemporary, becomes the reference point for declaring the social deprived of natural foundations, which makes speaking of radical reforms possible.

One of the defining features of civilization is that we are thrown into a secondary state of unnaturalness, and we are driven by a secondary kind of self-love (egoistic *amour propre* based on comparisons to others) rather than by the original *amour de soi*, which we share with animals. It means that whatever we do is marked by artificiality, even when we try to re-design politics and education so that they remain close to nature. Thus, the notion of nature as an original state tends to fall into the last of those enumerated by Baker: to something that can only be revealed *a posteriori* in man-made institutions (see the quote on Europeans, above). This means that the basic strategy we find in Rousseau is not that of return to nature, but rather of control and the diversion of the work of the supplementary, of the drive to self-esteem built on social recognition (*amour propre*), so that it eventually reveals the trace of the natural and works for the common good. However, this strategy is always secondary to natural law built on instinct and feelings, on *amour de soi* and compassion, or pity, which all humans have in their hearts (Baker 2001a; 2001b).

The aim of *Considerations* is consistent with that explained in *The Social Contract*: reconstruction of the law so that it meets the nature of men. As the text is targeted to a country rather than an individual, "men" are replaced by "the nation." Two issues need attention here. First, the nature of the nation (that what it actually is), encompassing its love of liberty, is itself a product of a given political system; it is, then, artificial. Second, it seems intriguing in what terms one can speak of the nature of a nation, as having its distinct, "inborn" features. In the tradition of political theory, Rousseau is associated with the trait of political (as opposed to cultural) nationalism. His nations are constituted in the course of institutionalization, which means that the bonds that unite people are political. This notion is opposed to that expressed, for instance, by Herder, for whom national bonds exist prior to the political creation of the state. They are grounded in the specificity of culture and, first of all, in language (Wiborg 2000). However, the excerpts quoted above seem to avoid such opposition. They situate the nature of a nation simultaneously within the "inborn" and the "political." The accident of birth throws us into a particular set of communicative practices and institutions that imprint on us their character. Whatever we choose to change in the course of social life has to take into account that "inborn" baggage which differentiates one culture from another. Natural (inborn) may have here, then, a double meaning: not only that which is born into us, but also that *into which* we are born. When we reduce the meaning of the natural to either of these dimensions, our reading of Rousseau becomes paradoxical itself.

There is one more dimension of nature here. Institutions that make people whatever they are may themselves be, or not be, pertinent to the nature of the nation. As Rousseau says, a failure to ground the organization of social life in nature (as I read it, in that specific, double meaning), produces despicable and dangerous sameness: "All [European nations] have the same tastes, the same passions, the same manners, for no one has been shaped along national lines by peculiar institutions" (Rousseau 1972, p. 5). Nations acquire their nature – that which makes them unique – by institutions that should be specific "to their nature," to that by which they already are unique. There is an idea that can grasp this peculiar sequence of substitutions: the Nietzschean concept that what is prior to what we are becomes visible only when it is subject to repetition, when it comes back displaced (Deleuze 2002). Rousseau's nature is always substituted, always supplemented by "another nature" that has to be artificially created for the elder nature (the "natural" nature) to speak or realize itself.

The program of education proposed for Poland, as Rousseau says, crucial to the viability of the political project, stems from the problem of political legitimacy, or from the tension between opinion and the law (Putterman 2001). In *The Social Contract*, the regulation of this conflict is appointed to the legislator, a nearly divine personality responsible for the first movement toward the law. The enlightening of the opinion in Rousseau's advice to Poland is speaking to the "heart" rather than to "reason." People should love the fatherland and its laws, and "the way of the heart" follows through a carefully staged spectacular pedagogy of political celebrations, through the construction of habits, and through popular games – an array of means copied from ancient regimes: "How then is it possible to move the hearts of men, and to make them love the father-land and its laws? Dare I say it? Through children's games; through institutions which seem idle and frivolous to superficial men, but which form cherished habits and invincible attachments" (Rousseau 1972, p. 2). The habits formed in games should, of course, be consistent with the "nature of the nation," that is, with those grounded in tradition. Properly formed, they will help to create the feeling of nationhood – and Rousseau speaks of it in a way that precedes the Hegelian dialectic of identity:

> [A] great nation which has never mingled too much with its neighbours must have many such [manners] which are peculiar to itself, and which perhaps are daily being bastardised by the general European tendency to adopt the tastes and manners of the French. It is necessary to maintain, to re-establish these ancient usages, and to introduce other appropriate ones which will be peculiar to the Poles. These usages . . . . will always have the advantage of making Poles love their country, and of giving them a natural repugnance to mingling with foreigners.
>
> (Rousseau 1972, p. 6)

The notorious circularity of nature reappears here like the undercurrent of political organization and education: "natural repugnance" should be "given" to people. In other words: when we construct common manners (collective iden-tities), we also construct aversion (difference) to the others. And this is "natural"; it grounds in the specificity of the nation. As I said before, after Trifonas (2000, 250), in Rousseau "nature works twice," through supplements and substitutions, and it is in supplements that its work comes before our eyes. So comes differ-ence. The "first difference" and the "first nature" appear only and inevitably in the context of their supplementation: as conditions of what is to be *constructed* as nature and difference. As Derrida says of such work of supplementation, in this sequence of supplementation there appears a certain necessity: "that of an infinite chain, ineluctably multiplying the supplementary mediations that pro-duce the sense of the very thing they defer: the mirage of the thing itself, of immediate presence, of originary perception. Immediacy is derived" (Derrida 1997, p. 157).

Children of (r)evolution

There are three ways in which *Considerations* is a pedagogical text. First, it designs a strategy for civic (republican) education. Second, the strategy of draw-ing the nation from where it is to where it could be is similar to that designed for educating Emile. These two pedagogies are different, and this difference is often noted by Rousseau researchers in reference to *The Social Contract* and Rousseau's paper on republican education written for the *Encyclopaedia*, on the one hand, and *Emile*, on the other (Osterwalder 2012). Third – this dimension has not been noted to date – Poland is constructed discursively in the position of the child, and, in some respects, a female child. I want to concentrate on the third issue as encompassing the other two as well. What I am interested in is the way in which the discourse of pedagogization, or the infantilization of politics, is constructed, and how it simultaneously works as a means for the naturalization of the previously constructed otherness of Poland.

The position of the child into which Poland is inscribed is marked by ambivalence and marginality. Being a child means being different, unpredictable, in transition, "neither–nor," half natural and half in the making, and outside of the dominant roles, rules, and meanings. A similar ambivalence is reported several times in descriptions of Poland. Marginality – being "outside meaning" – in a literal way means here being between the borders of the dominant meaning-making powers of the region (Russia, Prussia, and Austria) and far away from France. Femininity – like in descriptions of Sophy – is marked by weakness which is to be made empowering when Poland gains maturity. The country is *vulnerable, open* to invaders, and has to learn how to *play* with openness as her asset, eventually turning vulnerability into a trap. The female metaphor stops with the issue of identity. The vulnerability of Poland and the designed strategy of defense are "female," but the process of nation-making follows the pedagogy designed for Emile rather than that considered proper for Sophy. Nation-making may therefore be seen as both *aging* and *transgendering*, as a passage, or re-writing from the presupposed childish/female nature to male supplementation, from spontaneity and playfulness to institutionalization into the forms in which the displaced childhood and femininity will be retroactively discovered as nature.

The remedies to the problems of Poland have to be designed close to what she is – they are modeled on the experience of ancient peoples (from the time of Europe's youth), which she most resembles. Education, based on children games, should give the souls of Poles a national form, and all that the child experiences must support this form: "When first he opens his eyes, an infant ought to see the fatherland, and up to the day of his death he ought never to see anything else. Every true republican has drunk in love of country, that is to say love of law and liberty, along with his mother's milk. This love is his whole existence" (Rousseau 1972, p. 9). National education, like that of Emile, should follow the rules of negative pedagogy.

Poland should follow a collective strategy in educating her citizens. The crucial thing is to develop a common set of feelings, beliefs, and behaviors. This is apparently at odds with the commonly recognized individualism of Rousseau's education. As Osterwalder notes, the pedagogy proposed for Emile is different from that designed for republics, where citizens have to subordinate to the general will rather than following their own: civic education is aimed at public good and it has to be public. However, the difference is not as complete as this might suggest. Distinguishing between the program for the nation and that for her citizens, one should pay attention to the instance of *singularity* and to the subtle difference between a civic education and a national, political pedagogy. As I said, the nation – at least in case of the advice given to Poland – stands discursively in the position of the child, and in many respects the political pedagogy designed by Rousseau for Poland resembles that designed for Emile. But *citizens* should be brought up in a way which guarantees that they all love their state and its natural and political laws collectively.

> They should not be allowed to play alone as their fancy dictates, but all together and in public, so that there will always be a common goal toward which they all aspire, and which will excite competition and emulation.... Their instruction may be domestic and private, but their games ought always to be public and common to all; for here it is . . . a question of . . . accustoming them at an early age to rules, to equality, to fraternity, to competition, to living under the eyes of their fellow-citizens and to desiring public approbation.
>
> (Rousseau 1972, p. 10)

The singularity of the nation, resembling the singularity of Emile in the way it is treated pedagogically, needs to be created out of the plurality of citizens that should be brought to common behavior and emotion. Civic education must cater for the creation of the singular through the techniques of visibility and controlling the desire of approbation (*amour propre*). In *The Social Contract*, Rousseau says that the effect of the contract is that:

> At once, in place of the individual personality of each contracting party, this act of association creates a moral and collective body, composed of as many members as the assembly contains votes, and receiving from this act its unity, its common identity, its life and its will. This public person, so formed by the union of all other persons, formerly took the name of city, and now takes that of Republic or body politic.
>
> (Rousseau 1923, p. 44)

National pedagogy (politics of identity operating on a thus created collective body) aims, in turn, at *creating the different*, the specific, a nation unlike other nations. It is retroactive and retrospective, inward-looking, constantly concerned with "inner nature."

Education in general, designed in *Emile*, and civic education envisioned in *Considerations* may be seen as discrepant while referring to "man" and "citizen" (Wiborg 2000) or as "individualistic" and "collective" (Osterwalder 2012). However, this discrepancy seems to be apparent when we read the notion of nature as related to the singular (individual human being or individual nation) and to the plural. In the singular, nature stays dormant inside and has to be recovered. For nature to emerge in the plural, and thus to give it identity, singularity has to be constructed first, and it has to be grounded in something that is implied as already invisibly existing. While institutionally installed in the hearts of citizens, it works as the inner force (nature) of the nation that since then has to be respected in politics just in the way that the nature of the child is to be respected in education. Thus created, nations become children of their own nature (which is, in fact, a politically constructed difference against other nations), growing from the inside out, and their politics become pedagogical in the sense of Rousseau's negative understanding of pedagogy as preventing unnecessary deviation. Thus, through pedagogy, nature mirrors itself, asserts itself through repetition, but with the same gesture it questions its own naturalness. It looks at itself in a re-volved gesture. Nations invent themselves, and, in a proto-Hegelian manner, they thus become aware of themselves. They are children of their (r)evolution.

Rhetorics, politics, and education

The complex of ideas concerning the individual and the social in Rousseau circulates around the relations of nature, childhood, goodness, and divinity. The axes on which these relations are displayed are the topics of visibility and invisibility, of temporality (childhood, youth, aging, and infantilization, as well as the tactics of temporal encroachment), of deification and profanation, and of plurality and singularity. On a more general level, these relations are structured as the difference and the interplay between the ontic and ontological layers of theory. In the preceding sections, I have tried to analyze most of the topics above in detail. Some of them, however, need further explication. In this section, I will return briefly to the issues of deification, to the notions of visibility and invisibility, and to the construction of the ontic and the ontological. In the latter dimension, I see the answer to the question of the role of pedagogical rhetoric in the construction of the political in Rousseau.

The notion of the ontic/ontological difference is most commonly associated with Martin Heidegger. Ernesto Laclau uses it in relation to the ontology of the social rather than, as Heidegger does, to metaphysics in general. To give a very brief account of its sense, it speaks to the difference between that which can be expressed in the form of nouns (as objects accessible to our perceptions) and that which can be understood through verbs which depict processes rather than things and the becoming rather than the present in a given shape. To give voice to Laclau, it is about "the distinction between *ordering* and *order*, *changing* and *change*" (Laclau 2000, p. 85), while, and this is fundamentally important, processes are eventually conceived as invested in things; they cannot present themselves other than in the form of that which, so to say, crystallizes in the effect of their work. To use a Heideggerian metaphor, one can say that such processes (*Being*) "shine through" that which presents itself as *beings*, as things that are.

How does the ontological difference work in Rousseau's text, and what does it tell us about theorizing education? It speaks with two voices on two textual layers in *Emile* and in political texts. On the ontic level, *Emile* speaks of the world of, or for, the child. It is a world of spontaneous experience, of curiosity and scattered observations, of questions asked and answers heard, a world inhabited by friendly people and fascinating things. On the ontological level, *Emile* is about the laborious *production* of the former, about the teacher who works hard to *become* the appearance of himself, and still harder to control all other appearances displaying themselves on the scene of Emile's experience. A similar divide works in the political. The most striking instance of this is the work of the legislator in *The Social Contract*. As people are not social by nature and, moreover, their nature makes them unitary and, thus, self-reliable, which is at odds with the idea of the sovereignty of the people, the condition of building a social whole is to *de-nature* the individuals: to turn them into citizens. As Rousseau explains in the chapter on civic education in *Emile*:

> The natural man lives for himself; he is the unit, the whole, dependent only on himself and on his like. The citizen is but the numerator of a fraction, whose value depends on its denominator; his value depends upon the whole, that is, on the community. Good social institutions are those best fitted to make a man unnatural, to exchange his independence for dependence, to merge the unit in the group, that he no longer regards himself as one, but as a part of the whole, and is only conscious of the common life.
>
> (Rousseau 1921, p. 11)

The formation of such institutions cannot be undertaken, as seems obvious from this excerpt, by the members of the community as they are, not before they are transformed into citizens. And to be transformed, they should be shaped by proper institutions. This is why Rousseau introduces the legislator to *The Social Contract*. Apparently, his role contradicts the very task to be achieved − that of popular sovereignty. As Rousseau says:

> In order to discover the rules of society best suited to nations, a superior intelligence beholding all the passions of men without experiencing any of them would be needed. This intelligence would have to be wholly unrelated to our nature, while knowing it through and through. . . . He who dares to undertake the making of a people's institutions ought to feel himself capable, so to speak, of changing human nature, of transforming each individual, who is by himself a complete and solitary whole, into part of a greater whole from which he in a manner receives his life and being.
>
> (Rousseau 1923, p. 61)

Fritz Osterwalder (2012) says that while republican education continues the tradition of Humanism, the conception of education proposed in *Emile* continues the theological tradition. However, as illustrated by the excerpt above, the republican attempt at transforming individuals into citizens cannot escape theological language either. As John T. Scott (1994) argues, the whole political project of Rousseau is the imitation of the divine. This issue leads to that of invisibility discussed previously with reference to the invisibility of the preparation of the child's surroundings in *Emile*. Scott rightly observes that, just as in the case of *Emile*, the work of the legislator should not be visible to the citizens. It is focused on constituting "extra-legal institutions" (Scott 1994, p. 497), such as the habits of which I have spoken while presenting *The Government of Poland*, which are created beyond the range of public visibility. Rousseau says:

> I am speaking of morality, of custom, above all of public opinion ... With this the great legislator concerns himself in secret, though he seems to confine himself to particular regulations; for these are only the arc of the arch, while manners and morals, slower to arise, form in the end its immovable keystone.
> (Rousseau 1923, p. 72)

The work of the legislator, precisely like that of the teacher, is thus split between the visible (particular regulations in politics, or dialogs with the child in education) and the invisible (the formation of institutions, the formation of the teacher's *self* or of the educating environment) – "the extent to which the people are formed ... must be more or less unknown to them" (Scott 1994, p. 498). Importantly, to the reader of Rousseau's texts, and obviously to their author as well, these features form the ontological layer of the social; they are the conditions of possibility of politics and education alike. The issue of visibility and invisibility is, thus, inextricably connected to the figure of divinity, and it is in this tandem that the distinction between the ontic content of (projected) political and pedagogical practices and the ontological process of their construction can be arranged. It is important to note that the classic distinction between aims and means (of education and politics) is employed in the establishment of the ontological difference. While aims of education postulate the ontic (the granted, felt, unquestioned, natural), the means of education disclose the ontological: the very *constructedness* of human nature and of social compact. And it is on the level of means that the figure of the divinity, or authorship, of education and legislation dwells. No wonder that, to date, the *priesthood* is one of the leading tropics of teaching, as François Tochon finds in his analysis of contemporary educational debates. It is especially visible in education focused on freedom and autonomy. "Empowering others, [teachers] become stars by giving others a voice. ... But this paradigm also subjugates disciples and indicates what wrong thinking to avoid, it suggests what to think and how to teach, and points the masses down the path of righteous autonomy" (Tochon 2002, p. 32).

Still, the instances of divinity are multiple, and somewhat conflicting, which, rather than suggesting inconsistencies in Rousseau's text, may point to real tensions and the ambivalence of pedagogical and political work. On the one hand, we have clear references to the quasi-divine status of the legislator in *The Social Contract* and of the teacher in *Emile*. Both operate in a dual manner, overtly and in hiding. Both are also challenged in their quasi-divine operations by that on which they operate: by the divinity of the child and the divinity of the people. The first of these instances I have analyzed before, while the second appears in *The Social Contract* in a fairly open way: *vox populi* is *vox dei* – the general will of the people is divine. These colliding claims to divinity (the teacher/legislator working in the simulated position of God, in a deceptive way transforming subjectivities and polities which are also represented as divine) can be resolved when we place them on the axis of temporality. Education and politics are played in time, and they are linked in time. What is subject to change in time is, as said before, the relation between plurality and singularity of the objects of Rousseau's concerns. One may put these transformations in sequence. Starting with Emile, we have a singular, nearly natural man, unitary and complete; his initial education is organized so that the natural reveals itself, and the teacher expects it, he creates the conditions for the event of nature revealing itself. Then comes civic education (both in *Emile* and in political texts), where the singularity of man has to be broken and overcome. The society which is expected to emerge from the contract needs new, fractional subjects. Good institutions are, then, those which "denature" men and, while preserving their singularity while they are expected to vote, create the conditions for a totally new singularity to be formed. While the contract is made, "at once, in place of the individual personality of each contracting party, the act of association creates a moral and collective body . . . receiving from the act its unity, its common identity, its life and its will" (Rousseau 1923, p. 44).

The often noted discrepancy between *The Social Contract* and *The Government of Poland* may thus be explained not only by the need for singularity, of which I spoke before, but also by this temporality. While *The Social Contract* deals with a process of transition from a collection of individuals to body politic, to a common identity and general will, the book on Poland speaks to an *existing* nation-state; its system had become corrupt, but nevertheless it had been formed into a specific entity before, an entity which could not be mistaken for another one. Education, then, is split between that addressing plural citizens (their nature needs to be alienated and their identity needs to be linked to the collective) and addressing a singular collective of the nation-state whose nature has to be revealed by proper institutions creating or maintaining its mores and habits as unique. The transition from the singular/unitary individual (education in *Emile*), through the plural/fractional aggregation (denatured individuals investing their identity into the desire of collective identity) to the singular/unitary nation-state (Poland, the "contracted" society guided by general will) seems to sort the diversity of means proposed by Rousseau in a fairly coherent way. The ontological is thus organized by the tides, and relevant means of singularization and pluralization. This large temporal scheme is filled with micro-temporal tropes and tactics, like those of childhood and aging, of temporal encroachments (determining the future by controlling the time before the experience), and of infantilization as othering (in order to make room for the natural) and as justification of deceptive, manipulative work of invisible policies and pedagogies.

The same temporal scheme can be used to discuss the general status of rhetorics in Rousseau's work. As Benedetto Fontana (2003) notes, Rousseau follows Plato in his critique of rhetoric as deceptive. The general will acts as pure deliberation between individuals who should not, while voting, communicate with others. On the other hand, the only solution to avoid the use of force in the formation of society is through the use of rhetoric. This means that legislators need to communicate efficiently with those who do not follow their arguments, to be able to "persuade without convincing" in order to "move the masses" (p. 38). This is why the rhetoric of Rousseau's text is split – "the style and method of argument Rousseau uses in *The Social Contract* is not to be confused with the mode of persuasion that a political leader . . . would use when he addresses the masses" (p. 31). In other words, the founding act of society (the work of the legislator) must resort to rhetoric as means of persuasion, so that the common body is formed without the use of force. Once this is achieved, the general will should operate via the means of rational debate. However, the same distinction can be placed as operating on the ontological-ontic axis. Then one can assume that it is never possible to remove rhetorics from the political; that society constantly needs to be maintained by myths, stories, and opinion, and that these are constructed in ways invisible to the general public. In a systematic way, this idea is developed by Ernesto Laclau (see Chapter 6).

Notes

1   I follow Rousseau in his use of pronouns (usually male) when referring to human beings, also in my own text. Changing this convention would erase the fact that Rousseau'a vision of education for men and for women is radically different.
2   As Jean Starobinski (1971) notes, in his *Confessions* Rousseau tends to deny such revolutionary intentions of his political works. However, they are nevertheless *read* as such. As Baczko (1966) notes, *Emile* was one of the favorite books of Robespierre. The conflict between nature and culture can be overcome either by revolution, or by education, and both such interpretations find grounds in Rousseau's texts. Starobinski points to the interpretations of Rousseau by Engels in the first instance, and by Kant and Casirer in the second one.
3   Following the manner used by Rousseau, I usually use "Poland" as the name of the country, even though it was a commonwealth of Poland and Lithuania and its official name was The Republic of the Two Nations (*Rzeczpospolita Obojga Narodów*). For a more detailed historical context of Rousseau's expertise, see Szkudlarek 2005.

References

BACZKO, B. (1966). *Paradoksy Russoistyczne*. Introduction to: ROUSSEAU, J.-J., *Umowa spoleczna*. Warszawa: Państwowe Wydawnictwo Naukowe.
BAKER, B. (2001a). (Ap)pointing the Canon. Rousseau's Emile, Visions of the State, and Education. *Educational Theory*, 51 (Winter), pp. 1–43.
BAKER, B. (2001b) *In Perpetual Motion: Theories of Power, Educational History, and the Child.* New York, Washington, DC., Bern, Franfurt am Mein, Berlin, Brussels, Vienna and Oxford: Peter Lang.
DELEUZE, G. (2002). *Nietzsche and Philosophy*. London and New York: Continuum.

DERRIDA, J. (1997). *Of Grammatology*. Baltimore: Johns Hopkins University Press.

FONTANA, B. (2003). *Rousseau and the Ancients on Rhetoric*. Paper presented to the Annual Meeting of the American Political Science Association, Philadelphia.

FOUCAULT, M. (1995). *Discipline and Punish: The Birth of the Prison*. New York: Vintage Books.

HOSKIN, K. (1990). The Crypto-educationalist Unmasked. In BALL, S. (ed.) *Foucault and Education: Disciplines and Knowledge*. London: Routledge.

INSTON, K. (2010), *Rousseau and Radical Democracy*. London and New York: Continuum International Publishing Group.

LACLAU, E. (2000). Identity and Hegemony. The Role of Universality in the Constitution of Political Logics. In BUTLER, J., LACLAU, E. and ŽIŽEK, S. (eds.) *Contingency, Hegemony, Universality. Contemporary Dialogues on the Left*. London: Verso.

LACLAU, E. (2005). *On Populist Reason*. London: Verso.

LACLAU, E. (2014). *The Rhetorical Foundations of Society*. London: Verso.

MARSHALL, J.D. (1996). *Michel Foucault: Personal Autonomy and Education*. Dordrecht, Boston and London: Kluwer.

OSTERWALDER, F. (2012). The Modern Religious Language of Education: Rousseau's Emile. *Studies in Philosophy and Education*, 31, pp. 432–447.

PUTTERMAN, E. (2001). Realism and Reform in Rousseau's Constitutional Projects for Poland and Corsica. *Political Studies*, 49, pp. 481–491.

ROUSSEAU, J.-J. (1921). *Emile, or Education*. [Online]. Library of Liberty Project. Available from: http://lf-oll.s3.amazonaws.com/titles/2256/Rousseau_1499_EBk_v6.0.pdf. [Accessed: 15th September 2015].

ROUSSEAU, J.-J. (1923). *The Social Contract and Discourses by Jean-Jacques Rousseau*. [Online]. Library of Liberty Project. Available from http://oll.libertyfund.org/titles/638#lf0132_head_055. [Accessed: 15th August 2015].

ROUSSEAU, J.-J. (1972). *The Government of Poland*. Indianapolis: Bobbs-Merrill. [Online]. International Relations and Security Network. Available from http://www.isn.ethz.ch/Digital-Library/Publications/Detail/?id=125482. [Accessed: 15th September 2015].

SCOTT, J. (1994). Politics as the Imitation of the Divine in Rousseau's Social Contract. *Polity*, XXVI (3), pp. 473–501.

STAROBIŃSKI, J. (1971). *Jean-Jacques Rousseau. La transparence et l'obstacle suivi de Sept essais sur Rousseau*. Paris: Editions Galimard.

SZKUDLAREK, T. (2005). On Nations and Children: Rousseau, Poland, and European Identity. *Studies in Philosophy and Education*, 24, pp. 19–38.

TOCHON, F. (2002). *Tropics of Teaching. Productivity, Warfare, and Priesthood*. Toronto, Buffalo and London: University of Toronto Press.

TRIFONAS, P. (2000). Derrida and Rousseau: Deconstructing the Ethics of a Pedagogy of the Supplement. *The Review of Education/Pedagogy/Cultural Studies*, 22 (3), pp. 243–265.

TRÖHLER, D. (2014). Between Universally Claimed Theory and a Common Understanding: Theorhertical Knowledge in Education. In BIESTA, G., ALLAN, J. and EDWARDS, R. (eds.) *Making a Difference in Theory: The Theory Question in Education and the Education Question in Theory*. London and New York: Routledge.

TRÖHLER, D., POPKEWITZ, T.S. and LABAREE, D.F. (eds.) (2011). *Schooling and the Making of Citizens in the Long Nineteenth Century: Comparative Visions*. New York and London: Routledge.

WIBORG, S. (2000). Political and Cultural Nationalism in Education: The Ideas of Rousseau and Herder Concerning National Education. *Comparative Education*, 36 (2), pp. 235–243.

Chapter 3

Discipline, mechanics, and "the fluid element"

Herbart

In this chapter, I am looking at another founding text of modern education theory: namely Johann Friedrich Herbart's *Allgemeine Pädagogik aus dem Zweck der Erziehung abgeleitetet* (Herbart 1908). While the conceptual structure of Herbart's theory differs from that of Rousseau's, the figure of invisibility, as well as the connections between education and the construction of the body politic, play important roles here as well. They will be connected to the operation of discipline as formative of rational and moral subjects, and of the "science of education" itself.

The Discipline of education

Herbart was probably the most eminent advocate of turning educational knowledge into a distinctive academic discipline. In *Allgemeine Pädagogik* (*The Science of Education*) and in his other writings, he develops a conception of "general pedagogy"[1] that rests on three pillars: aesthetics as the knowledge of perceptions, ethics defining the goals of education, and psychology providing the knowledge basis for its means. In all these fields, his contributions were original and innovative. His psychology, for instance, foretells the contemporary cognitivist approach.

Herbart starts his argument for turning the knowledge of education into a distinctive academic discipline by distancing himself from former, practical ways of knowing education. Those who "wish to base education on experience alone" should look at natural sciences.

> They would then experience, that nothing is learned from one experience, and just as little from scattered observations; but that one must repeat the experiment twenty times with twenty variations before a result is obtained, which even then opposing theories can explain in its own way. They would experience then, that no one has a right to speak of experience until the experiment is completed, until, above all things, the residuum has been accurately weighed and tested.
>
> (Herbart 1908, p. 82)

Apart from postulating that the knowledge of education should be grounded in scientifically controlled data, Herbart insists that it is independent from other disciplinary fields. If we are, therefore, to know anything significant about education, we should secure a distinct and stable ground, a safe territory from which to proceed. Referring to the (then) negative example of medicine, Herbart says:

> It would be better if the science of education remained as true as possible to its intrinsic conceptions and cultivated more an independent mode of thought, by which it would become the centre of a sphere of exploration, and be no longer exposed to the danger of government by a stranger as a remote tributary province. Only when such science seeks to teach in its own way, and also with the same force as its neighbours, can a beneficial intercourse take place between them.
>
> (1908, pp. 82–83)

The reference to the model of natural sciences questions the style of pedagogical reflection known from Pestalozzi (whom Herbart admired) or Rousseau, which we might call episodic. Arguments are built there on the basis of realistic or fictional cases which introduce or exemplify rules believed to be universal. Continuing his argument against those who "wish to base education on experience alone," and referring to the idea of residuum that remains unexplained in chemical experiments, Herbart says: "In the case of educational experiments, this residuum is represented by the faults of the pupil when he has attained to manhood. Thus the time required for one such experiment is at least half of a human life. When then does any one become an experienced teacher?" (1908, p. 82). This comment clearly designates the role of the science of education as that of organizing cultural and historical experience, of shared memory and collective knowing, so that tutors and teachers do not have to rely on their always insufficient personal ones. Its territory should be distanced from other fields of knowledge, protected from their influence by the strength of its genuine concepts and systematic, cumulative research, and interacting with those other fields on its own grounds. What is needed, we read, is a new way of thinking of education that promises more effort and no easy solutions. What we gain is the possibility of thinking about education effectively, in a way that is specifically targeted for the purpose. Disciplinary autonomy is described here in the politico-geographical terms of nation-state independence, constantly threatened by stronger neighbors. Natural science, interestingly, does not seem to be included among those foreign forces. Some elements of the text point to philosophy, some other ones to theology as such threats.

The political metaphor, linking the discipline of education to the state, may be more than coincidental. As Bernadette Baker notes, modern pedagogies (like those of Locke and Herbart) can be read as "turning points in how new visions of the state become articulated as teaching techniques amid the perceived loss of theological certainty and singularity" (Baker 2005, p. 47). As she notes elsewhere (2011b), the movement towards the public school supported by the state was not so much a mark of secularization or an attempt at implementing social equity, as it was an effort to restore singularity lost in the wake of religious wars and the pluralization of denominations in Europe after the Reformation.

To turn knowledge of education into a science of education, one must make several assumptions. The first is that people are educable, that education is a process that is not impossible in ontological terms. In the context of the theological origins of pedagogical thought (Tröhler 2014), especially of the conception of the human soul as independent from external forces, it means that one should identify "the educable" *within* the human as well: a kind of mediating sphere which is open to external influences and which can, in turn, influence the inner spheres of the self. One should also envision psychological processes and pedagogical procedures of change that are grounded in the educability of humans thus defined. Let us note that, in Rousseau, this problem was addressed through the construction of nature as both foundational and incomplete, and thus needing supplementation through education. In a later text, Herbart makes a strong ontological claim on this issue.

> The first concept of pedagogy is formability of the child.
>
> Remark: The concept of formability has a broader meaning. It even extends to material elements. Experience shows that it can be traced down to those elements that engage in the transformation of matter in organic bodies. Traces of formability of will can be seen in the souls of more noble animals. However, the formability of will to moral life we only know in man.[2]
>
> (Herbart 1967, p. 24; my translation)

The notion of formability, or educability, constitutes the first tenet of Herbart's technology of the moral self. Morality is at the core of his pedagogy because to accomplish the human form of being, and here Herbart follows Kant, one must become a citizen. And morality has to be formed: the child is seen as empty; it has no natural goodness (as Rousseau's child had), no will, no inborn faculties. Herbart does not follow Kant entirely here. As Alan Blyth summarizes his argument against the notion of the transcendental subject in Kant, "if each individual child is transcendentally free, that is, if his volition is in fact something beyond the confines of the phenomenal world, then that volition lies outside the power of education" (Blyth 1981, p. 71). As Baker says (2001b, p. 383), "the tutor must start from the assumption that the morality of the child is within the tutor's control because the child is born without any significant power." This is why, for Herbart, moral education relies not on the categorical imperative (implying a formal capability allowing the subject to transcend her direct needs and make rational and autonomous decisions in moral questions), but on five moral ideas (of inner freedom, of perfection, benevolence, justice, and requital) which are directly, intuitively perceptible as "aesthetic necessities," in a way similar to the perception of beauty. As Karsten Kenkiles puts it, the perception of moral situations manifest themselves as "irrefutable judgments," and the task for education is to order these judgments by providing for the "right" perception of the world (2012, p. 271).

In other words, a child's perceptions have to be pedagogically organized to become aesthetically coherent and compelling. This demands the gradual, pedagogical construction of attention, of interests, of will, and, eventually, of character that will finally secure the cognitive and moral autonomy of the individual. Education has the fundamental role to play here, and the "aesthetic revelation of the world" (Herbart 1908) is the foundation of such education.

Herbart's theory is full of mechanical concepts, especially in his psychological descriptions of cognition and learning. In these investigations, which strongly resemble the approach of today's cognitive psychology, learning is constituted by movements of presentations; their complex relations produce "apperceptive masses" that actively work as cognitive structures against which new presentations are positioned and into which they are (or are not) integrated. This cognitive mechanics is paralleled by social mechanics. The five ideas of inner freedom, perfection, benevolence, right, and requital, mentioned above as concerning moral education, at the same time define the nature of the social (Blyth 1981). The condition of possibility for such social/individual coherence, as Baker notes, is grounded in the mechanics of the social that correspond to the mechanical nature of the mind.

This way of thinking, popularized in the wake of positivism, is characteristic in several respects. In a Cartesian way, it attempts to distinguish between the spheres of the subjective and the objective. This is why Herbart invalidates single experiences and scattered observations – they cannot stand the test of objectivism and they cannot produce laws that generalize cause-and-effect relations. However, strong notions of subjectivity and agency are also inseparable from such methodology. René Descartes started his journey into the method which long defined what science means, not from the realm of the objective, but from that which cannot be denied in subjective experience: from the act of thinking of the self-conscious subject. The definition of science is grounded, thus, not so much in the opposition between the domains of the knowing subject and the objective world, but in such a construction of the subject that makes subjective experience subjected to *the method*: to prescriptive regulations making singular experiences accessible to other subjects and repeatable in other circumstances. Scattered observations and single experiences are invalidated because they cannot contribute to the collective knowledge allowing for the predictable agency of other subjects who have not experienced given phenomena themselves. In this sense, Herbart is designing a *universal teaching agency*, an instance that transcends individual experiences through subjecting them to the scientific method. Such a "universal teacher" transcends himself as a particular person; he acts on behalf of the universal, and from the position of the universal. The teacher's action does not address the particularity of the child as well: "The teacher aims at the universal; the pupil, however, is an individual human being" (Herbart 1908, p. 113). Teaching does not engage the individuality of the student; it only aims at the *formation of the will* that will create a moral character that can free the growing person from the chaos of perceptions and blind fate. Pedagogy is humanistic technology, of the transformation of one state of the human (the chaotic, shapeless, uncontrollable, the falling prey of blind forces and fate) into another (knowledgeable, virtuous, capable of giving direction and meaning to his/her life, singular) by organizing the perceptions of the world.

In order to educate such humans, we need to know the laws that govern their becoming. Such dependence on rules is typical of technology as the end of scientific rationality. The rules of cause-and-effect relations are reversed and transformed into operational principles. From laws (in conditions C, A causes B) we turn to techniques (if you want B, create conditions C and let A work). Experiment is the main operational structure of such reasoning. Its power is grounded in the reversibility of relations between variables. The disclosure of cause-and-effect relations can thus immediately produce an accurate technological design. In Herbart's case, such relations concern human cognition. The movements of presentations (that which enters the mind as aesthetic revelation), their frictions and resistance, their aggregation into complexes (when they are not oppositional) or fusions (when they are opposites) and the formation of apperceptive masses which "gravitationally" attract other concepts – all these mechanics are summarized by Steinthal (quoted by W.T. Harris, the editor of the 1891 American edition of Herbart's handbook on psychology) in the sequence of identification, classification, harmonizing or reconciling apperception, and creative or formative apperception.

Let us add that the mechanics of presentations are the source of emotions, feelings, and the will – the whole psychic life is created and structured by this cognitive apparatus, by the movements, frictions, complications, and fusions of perceptions. As Blyth (1981) notes, the description of the movement between conscious and unconscious domains of apperception (e.g., Herbart 1901, pp. 11–13), foretells the work of Freud. This almost complete mental system, structuring itself in a manner resembling the contemporary notion of autopoiesis (apperception creates apperceiving factors) and open to the external world, devoid of inborn "faculties," is theorized in a way which allows defining education not as a supplement of the natural, like in Rousseau, but as the constitutive element of its self-realization. Education is *immanent* to the structural formation of mental system. It contributes to the creation of complexes of ideas or to their fusions; it structures cognition so that new presentations strengthen some elements of apperceptive masses and push other ones below the threshold of consciousness. It must, through its work on presentations and their movements, create *the will* which will complete the work of self-education, allowing for the construction of a strong moral character securing the autonomy of the person from being "governed by foreign forces," as we have read in the description of the science of education. This approach to moral autonomy as grounded in rationality extends the work of Kant by showing how external experience (and the experience guided by education in particular) contributes to the formation of the mind, including the formation of the categories of intellect. As Harris observes, "[i]f apperception is divided into two kinds – first, that dependent on the nature of the mind itself, and, second, that dependent on the acquired experience of the mind – then we may say that Herbart undertakes to explore the second field of apperception, while Kant explores the first" (Harris 1901, p. viii).

Herbart's reference to experiment as the methodological model for general pedagogy can be helpful in describing the relation between the "inner" and the "outer" (educable) experience. As I have mentioned before, the power of experiment relies, apart from its ability to control the variables and thus to model cause-and-effect relations, on its reversibility. If we know that under conditions C, agent A causes effect B, and if, by any chance, B meets our expectations, then we can easily transform the *logical* structure of the experiment into the *technological* rule of the production of what we want. Simply, one should create conditions C and let A work. We can link Herbart's pedagogy to his psychology of apperception in a similar way. His theory of instruction is the theory of the conditions of possibility, if I may use this Kantian phrase in a technological sense, of fortunate and ethically valuable creative apperception. The formal steps of instruction (where formal means content-independent) are: Clearness, Association, System, and Method (Herbart 1908, p. 126 and following). The ideas have to be presented *clearly*, then they have to be *associated* with the ideas the person already has, next they need to be harmonized with the system of apperceptive masses (where harmony creates positive emotions constitutive of interest and will), and the system is thus enriched and made operational in a way that allows for the creation of new ideas. If we recall the modalities of the Herbartian mind identified by Steinthal (in Harris, op. cit.), clearness in instruction results in identification in perception, association results in classification, system in harmonizing apperception, and method leads to creative apperception. The universal technological rule of instruction based on the scientific model of the mind is, therefore, the following: create *conditions* in which you can control what is presented and how it presents itself to the perception of the child (such conditions are achieved by discipline – see further). Then see to these presentations being clear, associate them with what the child already knows, try to harmonize the new knowledge with that which has already been obtained, and let the child use it in a creative, formative manner that produces new knowledge. The operative, rational, and volitional structure conductive of moral character will arrive in the mind of the child.

Herbart's theory has been criticized in numerous ways. The current dominant trait of critique was initiated by John Dewey. It refers to the issue of child's agency, but it also involves a very important question of how we understand society and what role it plays in education.

> The fundamental theoretical defect of [Herbart's] view lies in ignoring the existence in a living being of active and specific functions which are developed in the redirection or combination which occur as they are occupied with their environment. The theory represents the Schoolmaster come to his own. This fact expresses at once its strength and its weakness. The conception that the mind consists of what has been taught, and that the importance of what has been taught consists in its availability for further teaching, reflects the pedagogue's view of life. The philosophy is eloquent about the duty of the teacher in instructing pupils; it is almost silent regarding the privilege of learning. It emphasizes the influence of intellectual environment upon the mind; it slurs over the fact that the environment involves a personal sharing in common experience. . . . It takes, in brief, everything educational into account save its essence – vital energy seeking opportunity for effective exercise.
>
> (Dewey 2001, p. 76)

What is particularly important in this critique is its social dimension, the notion of the environment as involving "a personal sharing in common experience." Apparently, such a way of seeing society was not available in Herbart's time (Dewey's critique appeared over a hundred years after the publication of Herbart's theory), or it was simply at odds with how the transformational mission of education was then conceived. Dewey's criticism of the mind consisting "of what has been taught" finds, in turn, little evidence in Herbart's educational, and still less in his psychological theory. Transcribing this argument to more contemporary registers, I would rather say that Herbart presents a prototype of individual constructivism, while Dewey opens the gate for the social one. However, in the light of previous considerations, we see that the social (the "common experience") is present in Herbart's science of education, but it is not the Deweyan social. The main issue between the two philosophers is whether the social conditions of learning are or are not pedagogically controlled, and whether they should be so.

Science, discipline, and agency

In Chapter 1, I mentioned that the relation between Herbart's pedagogy and Foucault's genealogy of modern power was an important point of departure in my interest in political functions of theory in education. After the reconstruction of the basic tenets of Herbart's theory of instruction, a more detailed account of the ways these two perspectives are linked can be proposed. The main connection is, obviously, through the notion of discipline and its links to knowledge, subjectivity, and power – a structure visibly present in both Herbart and Foucault. This basic framework is complicated by features internal to Herbart's theory, like the structural similarity between the science of education and the child, or the foundational role of aesthetics.

In Herbart, discipline – an internalized government over children – is the condition of "educative instruction" that creates child's will. Government and discipline precede "education proper"; they are modalities of social relations. As I said, the social *is* present in Herbart's conception of education, but it is presented differently than in Dewey's. Its main appearances are normative (where Herbart speaks of moral ideas – the same five ideas shape the normativity of the social and the moral education of the child) and disciplinary ones. In the latter case, social environment is controlled in a way that makes the "aesthetic revelation of the world" possible and proper in terms of its educational impact. Government and discipline are socially constructed conditions of instruction: of clear administration of selected aesthetic experiences which can initiate the process of association, systematization, and creative apperception. Herbart begins his chapter on government with these words:

> It may be doubted whether this chapter belongs on the whole to the science of education, and should not rather be subjoined to those divisions of practical philosophy which treat of government in general. Care for intellectual culture is, in fact, essentially different from care for the maintenance of order. If the former bears the name of education, if it requires special artists, i.e. educators, . . . then we must desire no less for the good cause itself than for clearness of conception, that they upon whom devolves the task of training with their insight and energy the inmost minds of children, should be relieved from the government of them.
>
> (Herbart 1908, p. 94)

Of the aim of government, Herbart says:

> It is obvious that the aim of child-government is manifold – partly avoidance of harm both for others and for the child him self in the present and the future, partly avoidance of strife as an evil in itself, finally avoidance of collision, in which society finds itself forced into a contest for which it is not perfectly authorized. It all amounts to this, that such government aims at producing no result in the mind [. . .] of the child, but only at creating a spirit of order.
>
> (p. 96)

However, a moment later, Herbart mentions two "means of help which must be prepared in the children's minds themselves by government . . . : authority and love" (p. 98). These two means, or mediating instances, are also meant to precede "education proper." In short, government and discipline should be looked at as social practices of control making the work of knowledge and the formation of an autonomous subject possible. The difference between government and discipline lies with the locus of control. Government is external: the child must obey the tutor and follow imposed rules and restrictions. Discipline must be internalized. It has to work tacitly, usually unnoticed, only occasionally resorting to rewards and punishments, as if to remind the child of the existence of the force that brings order to the world. Also, it works deeper and involves instances that are not visible to external viewers and may not be fully accessible to the child subjected to education himself: "Government only takes into account the results of actions, later on discipline must look to unexecuted intentions" (p. 233). Interestingly, in the light of our "Foucauldian" minds, Herbart speaks of discipline as a hardly visible, liquid medium in which the growing subject has to be placed:

> In order that character may take a moral direction, individuality must be dipped, as it were, in fluid element, which according to circumstances either resists or favours it, but for the most part it is hardly perceptible to it. This element is discipline which is mainly operative on the arbitrary will (*Willkür*), but also partly on the judgement.
>
> (Herbart 1908, p. 120)

The "hardly perceptible" presence of discipline makes its results, and especially the will, habitual and hardly perceptible as well. Its work within the soul of the child is to be tacit, as if it were natural:

> So much is certain, that a man whose will does not, like ideas held in his memory, spontaneously re-appear as the same as often as occasion recurs – a man who is obliged to carry himself back by reflection to his former resolution – will have great trouble in building up his character. And it is because natural constancy of will is not so often found in children, that discipline has so much to do.
>
> (pp. 202–203)

We have to imagine Herbart's child as growing from the chaotic to the orderly; from being reactional to external incentives (not only those imparted in government, but, first, to spontaneous excitations and scattered attractions) to the ability of following his own interests and will. How does this relate to the construction of modernity?

As I have mentioned in reference to Baker, modern pedagogy and the state can be read as mutually related constructions: "new visions of state become articulated as teaching techniques" (Baker 2005, p. 47). Education, in political terms, is aimed at "making adults and children into the kinds of beings who could enact a social contract" (p. 58), which demands that human desires (the "wrong" ones, of which Herbart speaks justifying the need for government) are controlled and subjected to the desire of Utopia. Such aims are usually traced back to the Reformation (Baker 2005; Tröhler 2014; Tröhler, Popkewitz and Labaree 2011) as the driving force of modernization. More specifically, as Baker notes, the child is re-articulated from the theological "human by nature" (or by christening, as we see in Rousseau's departure from Christian theology) endowed with will that positions him or her as capable of good, towards an empty structure that has to be filled with perceptions, whose will and character have to be constructed. This is precisely the foundation of Herbart's theory. The state that is implied in this pedagogy is the one where religious particularism is to be overcome towards a homogeneous culture with a shared morality, where human behavior is predictable, and social differences are based on vocation (Baker 2005).

The predictability of behavior, which is related to strength of will and moral character, has to be secured by a "fluid," hardly perceptible discipline that conditions instruction, and, thus, education proper. This aspect of Herbart's theory sounds like a summary of Foucault's thesis on the productive nature of disciplinary power. The very sequence of government, discipline, knowledge, and the subject is easily recognizable as characteristic of Foucault's analyses. In other words, what makes Herbart's educational theory comprehensible as political is the very structure of its building blocks, identical with that disclosed by Foucault. As I mention in the previous chapter, the productive aspect of power is originally a Nietzschean motif, and if we follow its interpretation by Deleuze, it must be invisible to humans whose bodies and wills are formed by its meticulous procedures (Deleuze 2002). Such power must appear as subjectless: once it is invisible, we cannot say what or who the agent or the source of that force is. We just adapt to "it," much in the way we follow the Freudian *id*. Such productive, inward-directed force of reaction to that which is invisible, which is at the same time profane rather than divine, inscribed into the arrangements of space and naturalized as consistency of habitual behavior, seems to be the cornerstone for the project of modernity.

The rhetorical construction of invisibility of the active force in Herbart works through a homology between the two projects Herbart develops simultaneously: that of the science of education and that of its objects: of the child, the teacher, the domain of perceptions, and the system of knowledge. There are two, mutually related platforms of such a homology: aesthetics and the logic of discipline. Aesthetics, as the domain of perceptions, is the realm within which Herbart defines basic operations of learning and teaching. Perceptions in infants are originally scattered and driven by the objects themselves; they do not create anything that can operate as the concept of "the world" and produce a coherent attitude to it. Their chaotic presence has to be subjected to the ordering work of attention, interests, instruction, and will. Here, external influence (government and discipline) meets aesthetic necessity with which the world should present itself to individuality. A similar thing can be said about the relation between teachers' work and theory. Karsten Kenkiles notes that teachers are positioned by Herbart in a somewhat similar play of chaotic perceptions that demand ordering and discipline. Speaking of Herbart's notion of pedagogical tact as the instance which develops *via* practical experience and which tells the teacher how to mediate abstract statements of theory and concrete educational situations, she says that concrete educational acts cannot be deduced from theory (as much as moral behavior cannot be deduced from moral laws), therefore pedagogical tact must result from practical experience. The role of educational theory is, in this context, to provide for the *right perception* of educational practice "in the same way as education is supporting the pupil in perceiving the world in the right way" (2012, p. 271).

Teachers and children are thus immersed in the same structure of universal aesthetics of perceptions and subjected to the same universal logic of learning understood as disciplined and autonomous structuring of presentations of the world. The way autonomy and discipline are interconnected is, as I have already said, described in a way similar to that proposed by Foucault.

The argument for transforming the knowledge of education into a separate academic discipline is constructed in a similar way as that for disciplining the child, and it starts with a reference to disorganized perceptions. Like Herbart's child, the knowledge of education is described as unstable, vulnerable to the accidental and the irrational, and unable to control itself. Disciplinary procedures designed for the field of educational research, emulating those observed in experimental sciences, have to be internalized (by pedagogues) and are meant to lead to the autonomy of general pedagogy. Disciplining the knowledge of education means that observations and experience have to be accurate and systematic, subjected to the rigor of concepts that are specific to the discipline of pedagogy, and to the scientific, experimental approach to data and their generalization accumulating the experience of multiple researchers. Transferring Herbart's words describing formal steps in teaching, the science of education needs *clearness* (of methodical observation), *association* (collating singular data into larger sets), *system* (of theoretical concepts), and *method* (allowing for creative inferences, and, thus, producing new knowledge of education). The organization of experience in science installs instances similar to will, character, and autonomy into the knowledge of education itself, and connects it to the sphere of rational (rather than religious) morality, symmetrically to what education does to its children. In a way, Rousseau's gesture of personifying the effect of the social contract (a singular body politic with its specific identity) is repeated by Herbart in relation to science: discipline melts individual experiences into a quasi-political singularity similar to a nation-state operating against other states within clearly defined borders. In brief, it is no longer teachers or individual researchers, not even Herbart himself, who tell us how to teach: it is *the science of education* which becomes the elusive agent of educational knowing.

Reading Herbart's theory as involved in the rhetorical construction of invisibility of active forces, in spite of its undoubtedly rational character, exposes its apparently paradoxical aspects: the notion of imperceptible fluidity of discipline *evades* the methodological design of the science of education, which thus creates a sphere of invisibility within its very content. Invisible instances cannot be simply controlled as variables, and, thus, it is difficult to represent them "scientifically." This paradox can be resolved in Herbart's theory, as in Rousseau's, by distinguishing between the ontic and the ontological.

Invisibility: Ontological aesthetics and ontic mechanics

What this suggests is that the modern mechanisms of disciplinary power, of the dispersed and fractured governmentalities that permeate all aspects of everyday life, evade the structure of cause-and-effect explanations. Their disclosure (as by Foucault) will always be controversial as not meeting the expectations which give science its authority and political legitimacy. In other words, if modern mechanisms of discipline indeed operate as "hardly perceptible" (Herbart's words), or if force must be invisible (à la Nietzsche, Foucault, and Deleuze), how can one prove within the paradigm that they have been identified properly?

In a culture dominated by scientific rationalism, panopticism and dispersed discipline must remain elusive, felt rather than known, evasive of discursive thinking, impossible to be proven by methodologically reliable procedures, and eventually impossible to be controlled by the subjects educated under their influence. It seems, therefore, understandable that the disclosure of such dispersed social forces as political power was possible only within the postmodern turn in the social sciences: with both the attention and the desire shifted from the singular to the plural, from the complete to the always-provisional, and from logical coherence and systemic hierarchies to ruptures, discontinuities, and displacements.

However, in spite of the impossibility of subjecting the invisible to the rigor of experimental design, scientific rationality has always looked for invisible factors beneath the surface of phenomena, and since antiquity we have been able to infer their presence from observable indices. Moreover, science has been fueled by the hope of finding *the* invisible – the ultimate determining force behind the whole *system* of cause-and-effect relations. After all, modern science emerged from metaphysics and theology. Denying the divine as the ultimate source of everything, it replaced the "empty name of God" (Laclau 2014, p. 46) with empty explanatory structures in which profane (material, natural, or man-made) substitutive forces are searched for. Even though empirical sciences long ago forgot the idea of singular causes, the persistent need for logical coherence and theorization (or, nowadays, for singling out "what works") keeps fueling the drive to reduce the plethora of relations to maximally simple, "elegant," or manageable models. Jean-Francois Lyotard (1984) speaks in this context of the mythical foundations of science. Scientism is not alien to metaphysics: it delays it, postpones its ultimate questions, splitting them into ones made fit for empirical tests, as if with the hope that once we have verified them (or have failed to falsify them), a Big Synthesis of understanding arrives.

The search for ultimate causes, just like the search for identity, of which I will speak more in Chapter 6, appears to be both mistaken and irresistible, and we know many such constructions. The often spectacular success of their claims to singularity needs some attention here. Speaking ontologically, there is no single, identifiable "Agent A" fully determining the behavior of "Subject B." And, yet, the desire for singular cause-and-effect relations is still in place: it has been implanted into public discourse in the place that is traditionally occupied by religion (especially monotheistic religion), and from this place it acts as a privileged matrix of desire to comprehend reality. "Agent A," if not found, will have to be invented, hypostasized, crystallized in the empty space of providence and the final cause of human behavior. Social science thus produces *society* (or social structure, or the System) and imputes to it the feature of agency, grants to it subjective, systemic rationality that eventually works in domains previously occupied by fate, grace, or God's will.[3] Let us recall Rousseau's personification of the body politic emerging after the enactment of the social contract. This is how the longing for determinism can be kept alive, and this is why Foucault and other critics are often happily read as disclosing the secret plots of those in power to keep the masses in the darkness of panoptic visibility. In this interpretation, Herbart's general pedagogy can be seen as inviting a hypostasis of Society expected to fill the position of Agent A capable of determining the behavior of Subject B in our experimental metaphor.

The method of science, in the way it is described by Herbart, incapable of fully including the concepts of government and discipline in the body of the science of education (as a reminder, Herbart positions them in the margins of his discourse himself), makes political concepts both *foundational* to education and *impossible* to be included in the explanatory structure of its mechanics. The same method, by creating the structure of a chain of determination (x causes y causes z . . .), keeps science open to the old theological/metaphysical question of the *first* cause: and, thus, it invites, in the position of providence, the hypostasis of Society, or the State, as Baker has it, as the expected Agent of control, as the embodied force capable of forging Singularity, and embodied education capable of forming Characters. In other words, the mechanical and logical construction of general pedagogy foretells social determinism and the subordination of education to the State. The social dimension, identified by Dewey as absent in Herbart's theory, returns displaced in the form of "the state as a teaching technique" elevated to the hegemonic position of the "first cause," and the provider of inner freedom, perfection, benevolence, justice, and requital: of good society achieved by educational rather than revolutionary means. In the conceptions that will follow this trait of thinking, this hypostasis becomes a sovereign that demands loyalty and service, to whose anticipated needs we – the subjects – are expected to subordinate our lives. And, in the final steps of personification, it turns into a growing, desiring, ever-changing body whose autonomous movements (from "industrial" to "postindustrial," from "information" to "knowledge," from "teaching" to "learning". . .) define the goals of our own fluctuations, and we, as educators, follow and always lag behind these movements.

Invisibility and physics of educability: Mechanics, hydromechanics, and optics

The postulates of the invisibility of arrangements of the educational and political scenes in modern societies are themselves overtly visible in the analyzed texts. The texts need, therefore, to be read as split: they are not addressed to those whom they concern most, to children and citizens, and, thus, they mark the transition from priesthood (where the souls of those to be saved were addressed directly, in a persuasive manner, in the text) to profession. They speak to those who themselves will have to work so that the arrangements of the scene are concealed to those meant to occupy it. The professionals are taught how to create and manage the distinctions between the visible and the invisible. They have to split themselves, their own work and appearance, in line with such a distinction as well.

Nowadays, we usually associate the disclosure of such asymmetries in visibility with the work of critics like Foucault and Rancière, but, in fact, it is the founding texts of modernity themselves that make them apparent. The agents of modern power are postulated as invisible or split along the lines of visibility. Sometimes the authors of such texts speak of themselves: they not only postulate certain arrangement, but *design* them as well; and sometimes they disclose themselves in gestures of peculiar testimony. They may disclose their agency, and sometimes also their work of hiding it. Rousseau's legislator or his advice to those who would cater to the daily habits of citizens of Poland, Herbart's tutors who gradually turn overt force into imperceptible discipline, can, in this respect, be read together with Jeremy Bentham's design of *The Panopticon* – the project which equipped Michel Foucault (1995) with the guiding metaphor to define the modern power regime. As Bentham says, the Panopticon would gain its "ideal perfection" if each person was "in that predicament [of constant observation] during every instance of time. This being impossible, the next thing to be wished for is, that . . . he should conceive himself to be so" (Bentham 1791, p. 3). Both being visible and being *conceived* of being visible while one is not, as well as the invisibility of the guards which is the obvious condition of such conviction, are deliberately constructed as such – and, in this case, they are assigned singular authorship (Bentham mentions his brother as the author of this idea). The construction of the invisibility of control and of the (false and true) consciousness of being visible, and, most of all, of *the invisibility of the very distinction between visibility and invisibility*, are aesthetic and epistemological inventions permitting the internalization of the normalizing gaze.

In this context, we should point to an important feature of Herbart's text that is constitutive of the whole genre of educational writing. In spite of his fascination with empirical science, Herbart keeps using a language saturated with "should," "must," or "ought to" statements ("individuality must be dipped . . . in a fluid element"), which I call postulational rhetoric – in the sense of postulating which stresses the making of demands rather than assuming truth. This is clearly the language of *designing* the science of education together with its objects (teachers, pupils, minds, their perceptions, and their mechanisms, knowledges, moral ideas, etc.) and their relations. However, if we juxtapose his description of government and discipline with the fact that, according to Foucault, in Herbart's time disciplinary power was already in place and had the status of the dominant regime of control, the game between this existing regime of power and its *postulating*, or the *calling* for its existence in educational rhetoric, becomes a thing to consider. How can we read such statements in a society saturated with things they call for – as if they were not there?

A simple and important answer is that it is an operation of transposition, of a shift between the domains of the political and the pedagogical. In other words, panopticism and disciplinary control are parts of the daily regimes of power, but the language of educational theory transplants them into the realm of education, where they are apparently absent. The discipline of general pedagogy aims at overcoming the heterogeneous nature of experience (and, indirectly, of the social itself) through disciplinary practices and mathematical laws of mental mechanics. It tries to crystallize the flow of perceptions into discrete objects (the rule of *clearness* in instruction) whose movements are described as the mechanics of "solid" objects (concepts) which collide, form heterogeneous complexes, or blend into new entities. The dispersed, capillary, discursive formations of power/knowledge based on discipline – if we believe Foucault, prevalent in the time when Herbart was outlining his *Allgemeine Pädagogik* – are thus made invisible for this language as forces, just like pedagogical discipline, is claimed by Herbart to be "hardly perceptible" for the child. One may say that such dispersed forces are not "clear" enough to become valuable objects of perception, they will not be capable of construing *clear concepts*, and, thus, will not be applicable in the harmonizing work of cognitive apperception. However, one may expect that they will contribute to the construction of will and morals, but through behavioral habituation rather than rational cognition. Discipline becomes something fluid and elusive not only as a postulated manner of its operation, but also *because* of the logical structure of educational theory. Rousseau is more overt in this respect. His advice to Polish legislators includes children games as proper means of inculcating national habits in adults. Herbart's theory seems to make a different gesture. If we maintain the Nietzschean/Foucauldian vision of disciplinary regimes as being invisible, the fact of their overt description *as pedagogical*, and, thus, pertinent to children, may secure their invisibility in the political domain. As postulated, discipline is desirable. But postulated as the condition of *education*, it is desirable for *children*. It is thus infantilized, fixed in a marginal, politically insignificant position; even when spotted and interrogated, it will be seen as needed *ad usum Delphini* rather than as constitutive of political singularity.

Baker (2001b; 2005) often reminds us that behind the project of the modern state, citizenship, education, and childhood, lies the Newtonian conception of empty space filled with mechanical forces capable of transmitting the impact of one particle onto any other one which occupies that space. She defines the state as "systems of relations and methods of getting things done" (Baker 2005, p. 55). What returns in my analysis, though, are *fluids* rather than *particles*, and *influences* rather than *impacts*, as well as numerous instances of *visibility* and *invisibility* – in other words, "hydromechanics" and "optics," rather than mechanics. Such occurrences do not question Baker's observation: undoubtedly, Herbart's psychology, as well as social space in the common understanding of Herbart's contemporaries, are ultimately mechanical. However, in Herbart, the operation of the mechanical mind also demands optical and hydrological elements. Mechanical psychology allows for fluid discipline, but first of all it calls for it. Such transmutations are numerous. The optical logic of the Panopticon could be created only through the mastery in statics and mechanics of its architectural construction, which created the invisible optical conditions of visibility through which mechanical citizens (as singular particles moving in harmony to amass their force) could be produced. Such structural and temporal shifts between solidity and liquidity in the construction of social order are nowadays identified in revitalized "crowd" research (Lee 2014). Returning to the specificity of Herbart's project, fluid discipline operates as a hydraulic clutch between the mechanics of the mind and the optics of surveillance in the modern state.

Baker's definition of state is broad and simple, which makes it operational in her trans-historical/cultural contexts. We have to bear in mind, however, that such "systems of relations and methods of getting things done" crystallize as institutions with hierarchical power structures, monetary and economic regulations, military and police regimes, etc., which resist fluctuations of "relations" and "methods." Importantly, among these "things to be done," there is *The Thing* to be done. This *Thing* is the very "glue" of the social, capable of giving it precarious singularity (identity or totality, as Laclau calls it). The demand of this element sets into motion a mythical force that cannot be expressed in terms of mechanics, optics, or hydromechanics: it operates through *rhetorics*, through the operation of metonymies, metaphors, catachreses, and synecdoches (Laclau 2005; 2014). This issue is addressed in detail in Chapter 6, but three such rhetorical instruments can already be identified here. One is the desire for singularity located in the "empty place of power," which resulted from the revolutionary upheavals of modernity. Another is the operation of modern science, which "invites" the hypostasis of society as singular agent, even though its arrival is always delayed and deferred, and, thus, created as awaited; to transform a Derridean expectation of democracy (Derrida 2005), it invites a "society-to-come." Yet another is the complex tropology and the topology of invisibilities, evasions, and erasures that render force imperceptible – for instance by postulating that which already exists and, thus, making it virtually apparent, or by displacing it in a way which makes the mechanisms of power (which are invisible in politics) *visible* and desirable in education.

One might suspect that the proliferation of pedagogical discourse, where discipline and the transformation of soul are ascribed to minors, "frees" the adults of the sorry awareness of their constant operation on their own bodies and minds as the condition of their political existence. Education becomes a showcase of disciplinary power where technologies of pedagogical control and purposeful construction of the subject are experimentally designed and spectacularly displayed to the public. Children in modern states are thus becoming screens onto which political subjection is projected. The presence of schools with their visible governmentality attracts the public gaze like a red herring of the public scene, turning the eyes of the public from themselves to their children; from the center to the margins of the process of modernization. After all, modernity is about the production of future, and it is our children who are to be made responsible for its embodiment. Does this rhetoric of childhood as "the beginning" of future worlds make us, as citizens, alien in our political communities?

This hypothesis poses the question of the role of margins in power regimes. As Foucault says, technologies of power grow in the margins and are then utilized by power/knowledge regimes. Disciplinary power was invented in prisons, hospitals, barracks, and schools, and then it was appropriated, or colonized, as the dominant discourse of the modern regime extending it to the whole of the social. But perhaps the move from the margin to the center is doubled, repeated, and perhaps we will never know which of these momentums is the back-tide of which in their constant ebb and flow between the center and the margins. It seems, rather, that education and politics constantly work, in apparent mutual isolation, as respective marginalities. I am becoming more and more convinced that modern education is much more than a "tool" of political modernization. It seems to be productive not only of its citizens, but of its very instruments as well.

Notes

1   The concept of *Algemeine Pädagogik* has not been translated into English consistently. In the first American edition of this work, it was named *The Science of Education* (Herbart 1908). In the texts reconstructing German works on education for English-language readers in the last decades of the nineteenth century, the term *pedagogics* has probably been used most often (e.g., Schmidt and Haanel 1876; Ufer 1891). I am using the term "general pedagogy" which is currently used, for instance, by Bernadette Baker (2001b; 2005).

2   Originally *Bildungsamkeit*, typically translated into English as *educability*, and, except for this quotation, I am following this tradition throughout this text. The reason why "formability" is used here is because the term "educability" would not work in relation to physical concepts. The possibility of treating them as synonyms is grounded in the category of *Bildung* that can be understood as formation, as a process of giving or acquiring form, or shape. In this meaning, the translators of *The Science of Education* speak, for instance, of the formation of character by means of discipline.

3   This interpretation follows the scheme proposed by Claude Lefort (1986) in his analysis of republican politics as constantly striving to fill the empty position of the "head of the state," that was literally cut off during the French revolution. As Joan Copjec (1991) notes, all such replacements are quickly de-masked as usurpations, and pretenders become scapegoats blamed for the misfortunes of the people. The gesture of beheading has thus to be repeated continuously and usually in the ritual form of electoral campaigns.

References

BAKER, B. (2001b). *In Perpetual Motion. Theories of Power, Educational History, and the Child*. New York, Washington, DC, Bern, Frankfurt am Mein, Berlin, Brussels, Vienna and Oxford: Peter Lang.

BAKER, B. (2005). State-formation, Teaching Techniques, and Globalisation as Aporia. *Discourse: Studies in the Cultural Politics of Education*, 26 (1), pp. 45–77.

BENTHAM, J. (1791). *Panopticon; or, the Inspection – House: Containing The Idea of a New Principles of Construction Applicable to any Sort of Establishment, in which Persons of any Description are to be kept under Inspection: and in Particular to Prisons,, Houses of Industry, Work – Houses, Poor – Houses, Manufactories, Mad – Houses, Lazarettos, Hospitals, and Schools*. Dublin and London: T. Payne.

BLYTH, A. (1981). From Individuality to Character: The Herbartian Sociology Applied to Education. *British Journal of Educational Studies*, 29 (1), pp. 69–79.

COPJEC, J. (1991). The Unvermögender Other: Hysteria and Democracy in America. *New Formations*, 14, pp. 27–41.

DELEUZE, G. (2002). *Nietzsche and Philosophy*. London and New York: Continuum.

DERRIDA, J. (2005). *The Politics of Friendship*. London: Verso.

DEWEY, J. (2001). *Democracy and Education*. [Online] The Pennsylvania State University, Electronic Classics Series. Available from: http://www.naturalthinker.net/trl/texts/Dewey, John/Dewey,_John_-_Democracy_And_Education.pdf. [Accessed: 10th December 2015].

FOUCAULT, M. (1995). *Discipline and Punish: The Birth of the Prison*. New York: Vintage Books

HARRIS, W.T. (1901). Editor's Preface. In HERBART, J.F. *A Text – Book in Psychology: An Attempt to Found the Science of Psychology on Experience, Metaphysics, and Mathematics*. New York: D. Appleton and Company.

HERBART, J.F. (1901). *A Text – Book in Psychology. An Attept to Found the Science of Psychology on Experience, Mataphysics, and Mathematics*. New York: D. Appleton and Company.

HERBART, J.F. (1908). *The Science of Education. Its General Principles Deduced from its Aim, and The Aesthetic Revelation of the World*. Cambridge and Boston: D.C. Heath and Co. Publishers.

HERBART, J.F. (1967) Zarys wykładów pedagogicznych. [Polish edition of *Umriss pädagogischer Vorlesungen*]. Translated by B. Nawroczyński. In HERBART, J.F. *Pisma pedagogiczne*, pp. 23—182. Warszawa, Wrocław, Kraków: Zakład Narodowy im. Ossolińskich.

KENKILES, K. (2012). Educational Theory as Topological Rhetoric: The Concepts of Pedagogy of Johann Friedrich Herbart and Friedrich Schleiermacher. *Studies in Philosophy of Education*, 31, pp. 261–273.

LACLAU, E. (2005). *On Populist Reason*. London: Verso.

LACLAU, E. (2014). *The Rhetorical Foundations of Society*. London: Verso.

LEE, R.L.M. (2014). Modernity and Crowds: Solidity, Liquidity and Order. *Distinktion: Scandinavian Journal of Social Theory*, 15 (3). pp. 296–308.

LEFORT, C. (1986). *The Political Forms of Modern Society. Bureaucracy, Democracy, Totalitarianism*. Cambridge: Polity Press.

LYOTARD, J-F. (1984). *The Postmodern Condition. A Report on Knowledge.* Manchester: Manchester University Press.

SCHMIDT, K. and HAANEL, H. (1876). Herbart's Ideas on Education. *The Journal of Speculative Philosophy*, 10 (2), pp. 166–194.

TRÖHLER, D. (2014). Between Universally Claimed Theory and a Common Understanding: Theoretical Knowledge in Education. In BIESTA, G., ALLAN, J. and EDWARDS, R. (eds.) *Making a Difference in Theory. The Theory Question in Education and the Education Question in Theory.* London and New York: Routledge.

TRÖHLER, D., POPKEWITZ, S. and LABAREE, D.F. (eds.) (2011). *Schooling and the Making of Citizens in the Long Nineteenth Century. Comparative Visions.* New York and London: Routledge.

UFER, C. (1891). The Science of Pedagogics in Germany. *The Monist*, 1 (4), pp. 597–599.

Chapter 4

Education and the apparent society

As I argue in the previous chapter, the problem with the invisibility of modern power relations (as analyzed by Foucault) is reflected in the construction of the science of education (and social sciences in general). Discipline, with its fluid logic, cannot be theorized in mechanical language emulated after natural sciences. At the same time, this language allows for describing society (or the State) as the supersystem of hierarchic control, which thus becomes a hypostasis of the invisible power – and the abstract replacement for the overthrown, sovereign power of the monarch. The superposition of an abstract Society for the absent "Agent A" of disciplinary force thus follows the mechanical logic through which modern societies were imagined, but it cannot satisfy it entirely. Society is endowed with agency ("it" demands that we are rational, educated, etc.), and it, thus, becomes a signifier of elusive pedagogism, of discipline forming the subjects implied in the republican project. Owing to its singular form, it easily falls into the structure of technological thinking. It adapts to its syntax, it fills the positions of technological rationality with educational goals, means, and effects. Simultaneously, its fluid disciplinary logic is kept safely invisible by the very instance of scientific rationality. It is so because discipline/pedagogism lacks one of the most important features of agency in mechanical imaginary: it cannot be localized in time and space, its instances cannot be recognized as active force easily. Dispersed social control, fundamental for the operation of the political, becomes a discursively constructed undecidable of pedagogical thinking: it conditions its technical rationality, but it cannot be expressed in its theoretical terms.

In this chapter, I present a historical case which illustrates how a hypostasized Society can work as the ultimate agent of education.

Educating society

Scientific thinking shifts between the analytical and the synthetic, between pluralization and singularization. Herbart's pedagogy begins with a kind of experiential monadism (a solitary subject immersed in a chaotic environment of stimuli), at the same time developing a refined passage from plurality to singularity, from mechanics of plural presentations, through the creation of attention, interests and will, to a singular moral character of the self capable of changing the primary chaos into a meaningful structure. Herbart aims at reducing the heterogeneity of impulses by controlling their aesthetic revelations. This idea opens the way for the need to control *the environment* itself. Controlling the source of perceptions, rather than perceptions themselves, broadens the address of educational intervention from the child as a monadic mind immersed in aesthetic sensations, disconnected from conflicting communities of her or his socialization, to the child immersed in the social environment, and, consequently, to that environment itself. Such a shift follows the very logic of the "science of education" rather than its historical development. In fact, the process was not linear in this way. While Herbart was focused on controlling the input of perceptions arriving at the child's mind, earlier Rousseau aimed at creating milieus conditioning the child's experience. Anyhow, read together, these pedagogical strategies lead toward the need for managing the construction of society as the agent of education and turn toward its subsystems as targets of pedagogical intervention. Educational theory takes the position of the voice of the supersystem (Society) here, and from such an elevated position it can address particular milieus as objects of educational intervention. Altogether, this makes the relation between the social and the individual somewhat circular; it binds these two domains into a complex set of relations which re-articulate their mutual dependence, as if bridging their tension constitutive of liberal societies. This time, however, the unity between the social and the individual is made possible by situating them *together* as objects of pedagogical intervention. It is not only so that new social ideas need new pedagogically crafted subjects; the very task of education implies that the social itself, as the source of experiences and perceptions forming the child, becomes the target of education as well. Education assumes the role of time-space within which the social and the individual define their interwoven trajectories.

Leaving aside the long history of the idea of society, and of its being the agent of education, one may assume that its present form is related to republicanism, to the ideology of collective political will, and to mechanisms of restoring political singularity (or identity) after the revolutionary upheavals of modernity. With the introduction of the modern instance of "Society" and its placement in the position of agency, its subsystems (particular "societies" forming the one "with a capital S") could be ascribed pedagogical agency and eventually represented as demanding pedagogical intervention from those who claim to represent the supersystem. In brief, in this version of pedagogical rationality, if we want to influence the child, we have to perceive social milieus as *agents* of educating individuals and as *targets* of educational projects undertaken in the name of the social whole. Thus, what is created is a concept of *educating society*: the idea that children are formed by numerous social groups, institutions, and meanings that surround them. This idea builds gradually on Rousseau's pedagogical environmentalism, on Marx's (1845, p. 2) claim that "the essence of man is no abstraction inherent in each single individual [. . . but] it is the ensemble of the social relations," on Dewey's (2001) understanding of personal experience as embedded in the social/historical one, on Mead's understanding of the self as "an eddy in the social current and so still a part of the current" (Mead 1934, p. 182), and on numerous instances of social/cultural constructivism. As long as scientific rationality finds its fulfillment with the creation of systems, heterogeneous milieus perceived as surrounding individuals and determining their education provoke a move toward their conceptual concentration, coordination, and integration; a search for some underlying or emergent unity. Of course, this ideal is not a modern invention; it is grounded deeply in the history of educational utopias. However, its *scientific* incarnation is clearly the product of modernization, of institutional changes that eventually led to the idea that *the whole* of social experience is pedagogically significant and, consequently, that it would be good if it were controlled pedagogically.

In the following, I analyze the mature articulation of this idea expressed in the first volume of Florian Znaniecki's *Sociology of Education* (1973, first published in 1927[1]) entitled *The Educating Society*, and in its appropriation as one of the headlines of Polish educational policy after the political crises of the (then) socialist state in 1968–70. Znaniecki's "educating society" denoted a *fact* of social life. Every social group, driven by the need for self-sustainability, strives to recruit new members and make them useful to the group. This is the social foundation of education. In modern societies, individuals are immersed in dense networks of groups and are, thus, surrounded by conflicting influences that compete for their identification. Education is, thus, the business of social groups and societies rather than that of individuals. Znaniecki makes a distinction between education and self-education, the latter being solely responsible for the growth of individual personality, and also for creative or prospective aspects of education. Education "proper" is concerned with *social* personalities, with those aspects of human life that are important for the sustainability and development of groups and societies. Summarizing his analyses of educating society in the second volume of his *Sociology of Education*, Znaniecki says:

> We have seen that every relatively stable group, concerned with securing the inflow of new members, demands of these newcomers that they are capable of participating in its communal life. Every new member has to go through a period of candidacy when his capability can be tested and faults corrected in special preparation. That preparation for membership in the term of candidacy is the source and remains the social function of education.
>
> (Znaniecki 1973, p. 47, my translation)

The goals of education are conditioned by future duties of group members. All those duties have one more, more remote and common task: to sustain the group, or the system of groups organized in a society. Therefore, because of its social function, education must be analyzed in connection with social groups and in their territories.

(p. 49, my translation)

Social systems are complex. Znaniecki discusses at least four kinds of heterogeneous "societies" that interact in the same territory: national, state, religious, and class societies, each of which is composed of numerous groups. It is these groups and societies that are the *agents* of education, that formulate goals and invent strategies for the formation of the young so that they meet the needs of particular forms of social life. As Jan Szczepański notes in the foreword to the 1973 edition of Znaniecki's work, his way of analyzing society foretells the systemic approach, later elaborated by Talcott Parsons (1951), which dominated social sciences in the 1960s. In a way, this classic sociological text foretells contemporary studies on identity (e.g., Giddens 1991) as well. It is the individual, belonging to numerous groups and societies and to none of them fully, who has to recollect conflicting traits and pressures into her/his social identity.

As I have said, Znaniecki's notion of educating society is descriptive, as it defines the origins and the nature of education. In other words, societies *are* educating entities. However, Znaniecki is concerned not only with what societies are, but also with how and what they become. In the last chapter of the first volume of *Sociology of Education* and throughout the second one, his language changes, and it becomes saturated with postulates typical of pedagogical discourse. Znaniecki speaks of perils and threats facing Western societies. The tragedy of World War I bitterly foretells what will happen in the next war to come. Against this fate, societies must work toward two goals: replacing the logic of conflict and war with that of cooperation, and overcoming natural conservatism so that their evolution is controlled rather than resulting from accidental challenges. Societies change, and in their mature form they must predict and actively shape these changes. The only way to achieve this is through the education of individuals ("positive deviants" or "super-deviants") capable of formulating visions of the future and inspiring groups and societies to enact them. Education acquires its utopian and progressive dimensions here.

After the Second World War, Poland fell under Soviet domination: a powerful Soviet military contingent was stationed in Poland, and Soviet officials controlled the politics of the country. Educational policies served the questionable legitimacy of the ruling Workers' Party, the power of which was maintained not only by cultural and political hegemony, but by military and police force as well. One such legitimizing issue was social justice, which indeed led to the greater accessibility of education for traditionally underprivileged social groups. Education also served the needs of "heavy" industrial modernization (an efficient vocational education sector), and it was used to create *singularity*, or national and political unity, which, in the context of post-war instability and radical political changes, was the most important aspect of state propaganda and cultural policy. This issue was extremely important in educational policies. The results of WWII, including the horror of the Holocaust and the re-drawing of the borders and of the ethnic composition of the state, were represented as tragic and as the reason for active peace politics (in its version enforced by the USSR), but at the same time the tragedy was "consoled" by proclamations of national unity. One could find such "but" rhetoric in newspapers and history textbooks easily: Poland lost a large proportion of her population and her historically significant territories, *but* she became an ethnically homogeneous country. Such homogeneity was represented as invaluable, but constantly threatened by the perspective of ethnic Germans returning to their homes left in the western provinces of the new state, which construed the constant presence of the Soviet Army as necessary for Poland's security. In this context, national unity worked as a concept justifying the eradication of "dangerous" memories (like those of the Soviet occupation or of the Katyń massacre of Polish officers) and of "dangerous" plurality and dissent. Its pedagogical construction was harmonized with cultural policies, political propaganda, and the means of enforcing consent in daily politics.

In spite of the orchestrated effort to build the singular, post-war politics in Poland were marked by eruptions of rage. As democratic dissent was impossible, antagonisms recurrently erupted in violent riots. The 1973 edition of Znaniecki's book on educating society appeared after two such eruptions: in March 1968, Polish students rebelled against censorship and cultural politics and were quickly accused of threatening national unity and of ignoring the benefits of free education provided by a state claimed to be ruled by workers. Workers were therefore organized by the Party to protest against students and their academic teachers. Under this pretext, numerous academics and intellectuals were arrested, and those of Jewish origin were often forced to leave the country. Organized anti-intellectualism and anti-Semitism was employed as the means of reconstructing national "unity" after the rebellion through the construction of its "constitutive outside," in Ernesto Laclau's terms (Laclau 2005; see Chapter VI). In August 1968, as if to reassure the Soviets of Polish loyalty, the Polish army assisted the USSR in crushing political reforms in Czechoslovakia. In December 1970, shipyard workers in Gdańsk and other northern cities rioted against ineffective economic policies. The students remained silent. The riots were crushed violently by the police and the army, and after the death toll was made public, the ruling party changed their leaders and a new government started to work to modernize the country and to gain public support. Singularity, shattered by pitting workers against intellectuals and by all of them rioting against "the System," became the central issue again.

These efforts were widely influential on educational policies. The main rationale behind the reforms undertaken in the 1970s was based on the assumptions of General Systems Theory (GST), then one of the dominant paradigms in social sciences. Education was defined as a subsystem of society, and its functions were defined within this framework. The design of the new school aimed to optimize all areas of educational influence. One of the most interesting developments was understanding schools as hubs coordinating networks of learning resources and of forces active in the construction of social identities. Professional counselors were trained and employed to coordinate this, and the policy was aimed at every public institution having its educational officers. Teachers were expected to play active roles in their communities (e.g., as social workers, sports instructors, cultural activists, etc.), and schools were obliged to make their facilities accessible to locals. They cooperated with culture centers, family courts, youth organizations, the police, and sports clubs. They were supposed to be active in crime prevention, public health, to cooperate with local factories, housing associations, local administration or planning authorities (for instance, in translating planned demands for workforce into vocational counseling); also with the military or with psychological consultancy services. Thus, the child was surrounded by a dense network of institutions and services, the center of which was the school where all possible influences converged, were recognized, and coordinated. The systemic approach meant that all public institutions, neighborhoods, and families were seen as contributing their specific "educational outcomes" to the holistic, life-long formation of members of the socialist society. Schools were tasked with monitoring and integrating such partial influences. In some respects, the language of such projects was similar to the contemporary discourse of life-long learning and to the policies of recognition of prior and parallel, extra-school education (cf. Szczepański 1975). Some authors, though, employed military rhetoric and spoke of a "unitary front of extra-school education" in which schools were given the leading role, and they warned against "extremist" conceptions (e.g., Ivan Illich's idea of de-schooling society) that "create delusion and chaos in the opinion of the broad public" (Wołczyk 1974, p. 37). The system – along the lines of the then globally fashionable general systems' theory, mixed with the ideology of state socialism – *must* be hierarchically controlled, functional, and, obviously, singular.

In the foreword to the 1973 edition of Znaniecki's book, Jan Szczepański links the Polish events of 1968 to the global rebellion of the young:

> In the 1960s, we witnessed a . . . crisis of educating society. This means diminishing, and in many societies on a significant scale, the ability of societies to guide their young generations towards established ways of behaving and recognizing values achieved by their senior generations. That "natural" process of . . . socialization and education was interrupted by negativism, or even by the rebellion of the young. . . . Hence the growing interest in the problems of education, and the careful scrutiny of all educational institutions which are usually charged with responsibility for the events that by some people are seen as threatening the cultural sustainability of societies. I think that we have to see the work of Znaniecki in this context.
>
> (Znaniecki 1973, p. VII, my translation)

Praising the quality of Znaniecki's theory, Szczepański underscores its pioneering character in systems analysis. He also notes that education in Znaniecki is a social process, which means that it is complex social settings rather than individuals that are the agents of education. Elsewhere (Szczepański 1975, p. 32), Szczepański notes that the idea of educating society is embedded in the work of Marx. He also points to Znaniecki's conception of subjective agency, to his focus on aims rather than means of education, to his critique of isolation of the school from everyday life, and his theory of social milieus of which the school is an element. All these qualities, as we read in the passage quoted, are employed in the service of cultural transmission threatened by the rebellion of the young.

The 1973 publication of Znaniecki's book was not merely aimed at repairing the damage caused by the rebellion. It was meant to inspire systemic reforms in education as a factor of planned modernization. The reforms were supported by think tanks led by the "Poland 2000 Committee" at the Polish Academy of Sciences, in an attempt to ground the directions of change in future research. Znaniecki's idea of educating society became one of the catchwords in their blueprints for an integrated system of education.

Employing Znaniecki's term as part of the agenda of modernization and of the pacification of dissent resulted in changing its ontological referent. In the pedagogical literature typical of the time, the notion of educating society shifts from descriptive to value-laden, postulational meaning: from the present heterogeneous "which is," to the future homogeneous "which should be." Even though the notion of communism was never used in state policies, the utopia of the great commune was evidently in the back of the heads of the political elites. As I have said before, this rhetorical shift (without a totalitarian background) was initiated by Znaniecki himself, in his turning from sociology to pedagogy and from descriptive to postulational language. This shift was repeated in the 1970s, when educationalists, sociologists, politicians, and journalists debated intensively modernization, civilization gaps, future management, and preventing the young from deviating from such worthy aims. In the opening address to the 1979 conference devoted to this issue, Bogdan Suchodolski recognizes the changing meaning of the term:

> Commonly used since the time of Florian Znaniecki, the term "educating society" initially had a descriptive rather than normative meaning. It referred to any kind of education realised by social groups and in social situations. Nowadays, however, there is a tendency to use the term in a value-laden manner. Society is considered to be the institution of valuable education rather than a composition of groups moulding their members.
>
> (Suchodolski 1983, p. 7, my translation)[2]

The paper by Andrzej Siciński (1983) in the volume of conference proceedings, where the idea of innovative education is presented as a means to achieve the "desirable society" defined in terms of systemic optimization, is a good illustration of this tendency. Shifting from description and analysis to the exposition of a "desirable society" as the end of human action inevitably involves a rhetorical shift. The rhetoric of such postulates and their ideological functions was addressed at the same conference by Jan Strzelecki, who analyzed the status of the key symbols of that discourse. Strzelecki (1983) also reminds us that Znaniecki used the notion of educating society in a descriptive sense, which in the context of contemporary knowledge – as Strzelecki argued – was no longer original; in other words, the descriptive potential does not explain the return to Znaniecki's theory in the 1970s. However, the same concept reveals a lot when analyzed in its normative aspects in the specific context of the time. Here, educating society is very often identified with a *socialist* society (cf. Szczepański's observation of its Marxist provenance, above); thus, it becomes an "all-inclusive dogma" that overshadows the complexities of the social. What is crucial here is the very proclamation that *socialism* is *education*.

> It seems that in contemporary texts, in which the notion of "socialist society" takes the place of "educating society," there are numerous representations ... that qualify those texts to the genre which I call *all-inclusive-dogmatic*. Such qualification is evident in the case of texts in which the real system of social processes and institutions ... is presented as the field of inevitable realization of all humanistic values, as the space in which the most ideal of human communities is being incarnated, and in which the proponents of the case, as representatives of "educating society," are entitled by the very perfection of their intent to manage all aspects of the body and soul of their subjects in constant, caring tutelage. Such a conceptualization of "educating society" gives its content an all too sacred character, and positions its proponents as the sole intermediaries between the human and the world of values.
>
> (Strzelecki 1983, pp. 21–22, my translation)

Strzelecki reveals a religious rhetoric embedded in the discourse of, apparently lay, socialist education under Soviet domination. What he refers to can be understood as a movement of elevation and return, of "abstraction" and "falling back," as Gilles Deleuze and Felix Guattari (2004) call it in their reference to Marx's critique of capital. Reality is colonized by its own abstraction, by an element which derives from it and "falls back" on its surface as its "concept," and its proponents claim that reality must comply with its logic. The high value of educating society is abstracted from social practices and it "falls back" on them so that they have to comply with its sacred authority. No longer is "educating society" a mere description of practices of competing social groups; it becomes a dignified process of *Bildung* through which society is meant to become truly human, or indeed to become "itself," a being identical with its essence. Thus elevated, it gains spiritual esteem that sheds light on concrete practices and policies, giving them a spiritual dimension and making their intent perfect and, thus, unquestionably legitimate. The sacred character of this sublimation and its falling back on the mundane is couched in a language typical of religious mysticism, where the subjective and the objective and the *Sein* and *Sollen* (being and value) are no longer distinguishable. In an example of this language, given by Strzelecki, we read: "Socialist humanism realizes the highest social values as the features of the objective world it creates. . . . The objectively existent material sphere of social life becomes the vehicle and the ultimate source of values" (Strzelecki 1983, p. 22).

Strzelecki notes that neither the descriptive (as in Znaniecki) nor the "all-inclusive-dogmatic" approach to educating society is sufficient to analyze the social. Both of them erase the *problem* of the goals of education, and they make the debate on the aims and reasons of educating redundant or impossible. Analyzing the debate on educating society in the 1970s, especially the educational report written by a committee headed by Jan Szczepański (Komitet ekspertów . . . 1973), Strzelecki identifies, as the key symbol of that document, the notion of socialism as "the social system built by people for the people" (p. 24). This empty signifier permits articulating popular participation in managing social issues, overcoming alienation and indifference, and replacing enforced subordination of individuals with their subordination by will. This pedagogical reformation is believed to liquidate inequalities, to eliminate unqualified labor, to blur the distinction between manual and intellectual work, and, finally, to integrate social and personal interests into one, enlightened totality.

One may read this case as the illustration of how theological language permeates and informs modern governmentality in a regime whose power is consequently dissolved in daily pedagogies cutting through all practices of social life. In this rhetoric, the idea of educating society mixes the technical language of science (in this case, that of General Systems Theory) with the Hegelian logic of *Aufhebung* that overcomes all contradictions of the social. Educating society is an incarnation of a desired condition in which young generations may both adapt to the existing social system and creatively engage in its transformation. The idea of education is, thus, extended to the whole of social experience. Even though such a postulate employs technological rhetoric, and although numerous attempts at building coordinated networks of education and cultural work in factories, neighborhoods, etc., were really taken up in the Poland of that time, "educating society" was not only a goal that was technically realized in educational practices, but also, and foremost, an empty signifier that gave mystic coherence to political and theoretical thinking of education, becoming – after its "falling back" on the surface of the social – an ideology that gave legitimacy to often controversial institutional practices. As Slavoj Žižek notes, ideology works as a *positive force* that gives reality its coherence and comprehensibility. Its operation, in this understanding, becomes the crucial factor in the strife for singularity, or for social identity (Žižek 1989). On the other hand, educating society in its version proclaimed in the 1970s in Poland, as a sacred incarnation of the ideal, appears to be an ecstasy (in Baudrillard's terms 1983) of illusory being, a simulation of itself, something that revolves around itself and comes back to itself without any dialectic tension, without dynamic that would make it productive in providing ideas capable of understanding the social. It became an empty phrase substitutive for the name of the social itself (cf. its equivalence to socialism), and, thus, it could play its ritual role in legitimizing the system "through the perfection of its intent."

The shift from the (empirical) real in descriptive, sociological approaches to the ideal, mystically pedagogical way of writing in socialist Poland was, to some extent, a direct consequence of Marxist and, thus, indirectly, Hegelian logic. "Before" it becomes a simulation of itself (or immanence), the notion of educating society is construed as dialectically overcoming the tension between the social and the individual; it bridges educational subjectivism and objectivism and creates a horizon of integrity. On the other hand, it has a material dimension. Educating society is a product of absolutely real practices of erasing social differences in a totalitarian political routine, of political control of curricula and institutional coordination of what we nowadays call learning outcomes. Both its conceptual logic which results in the collapse of values into the real, and its institutional practices of controlling extra-institutional learning mean that the value of critique, the need for distance to reality becomes elusive. The all-inclusive dogma meets all-inclusive practices of educating. The fullness of society is proclaimed in the act of the *return of the ideal*, first abstracted and expropriated, then restored, "fallen back" on reality as its dignifying logic. Like neoliberalism in the proclamation made by Fukuyama (1992), then bureaucratic socialism was thought to end the history of striving for good society. If reality is *complete*, what we can do in education is just make the young submerge in it. Let us note that any proclamation of the end of history must be threatening to education, it must turn its language into the mix of technical trivia and the mystic aura of fullness maintained by ritual chanting, *re-enchanting* reality in repetitive declarations of *Aufhebung*. Such language legitimizes reality in its *actual* shape by giving it a comprehensible structure and the ultimate meaning of historical necessity. At the same time, it hides the very nature of that reality; it deprives it of signifiers that could be related to its conflictual, antagonistic, never complete social fabric. It is worth recalling in this context, after Rousseau, that education is *supplementary*, that it is grounded in the *incompleteness* of the human and the social. The mystical language turning mundane pedagogism into the ecstatic fulfillment of the desire of fullness makes *factual* operations of total control over the social incomprehensible *as political* and as a subject of critical interrogation.

Reality and appearance

An interesting interpretation of the "problem of socialism" in its Soviet-controlled incarnation, which, in my opinion, is far more universal than such a historical context suggests and can, thus, be read as pertinent to all purposefully designed social systems, is found in the paper by Jadwiga Staniszkis from 1987, which was later elaborated into a book on the ontology of socialism (1992). Staniszkis tries to distance herself from the tradition of thinking of socialism in Eastern Europe in terms of *lack* (as a system "without" democracy, choice, private property, etc.), and interrogates positive qualities of that form of polity. She uses the conceptual framework of Hegel's *Science of Logic* (Hegel 2010), analyzing socialism as *apparent being* that cannot be explained, or understood, in terms of its premises. The reason for such an impossibility lies with the very logic of essence. Our cognition separates essential and unessential momentums of reality based on concepts referring to these essential dimensions. These concepts are used to describe reality and, still more importantly, to act in order to accomplish its logic, to fulfill its essence. However, acting according to concepts and, thus, ignoring unessential aspects of things, we create illusory beings. Such illusory status results from the fact that, in actuality, beings are composed of both essential and unessential elements. All these aspects interact and produce complex results that are impossible to understand solely in light of what we conceptually grasp as essential. Coming back to socialism, its reality (its *immediate existence* in Hegel's terms) is, in light of what we are capable of knowing, illusory (apparent), i.e., it appears as a "fake" reality. In other words, the immediate (or empirical, in more contemporary language) existence of a socialist state cannot be explained *as socialism*: socialism created on the premises of socialist ideas *is not socialism*. What exists there immediately results from complex interplays between comprehensible (essential) and unrecognized, unessential features, and it needs another set of ideas, another conceptual framework to be understood: it cannot be explained in terms of socialist ideals any more.

Moving towards the analysis of the particular form of socialism in pre-1989 Poland, Staniszkis presents the following dialectic of essence and appearance. According to the ideal, socialism is a system where economy is based on collective ownership (meant to overcome capitalist exploitation and alienation), where politics are based on the identity (or historical mission) of the working class, and on popular agency. On the level of appearance (i.e., in the "immediate reality" built on such premises), this idea results in economy without economic subjects, in the lack of civil society, and in substituting the lack of property and economic agency with administrative control. On the political side, the power in this illusory being works *without politics* (no articulation of antagonisms, interests, etc., is possible – cf. the role of the desire of singularity discussed before), and it is based on the self-declared leadership of the Party (*nota bene*, this is how the desire of the singular worked in political rhetoric: the full name of that ruling organization was Polish United Worker's Party; it was not the only party on the scene, but it was "elevated to the dignity of the Thing," to use a Freudian phrase in the sense given by Ernesto Laclau (2005), and was commonly called *The Party*).

As a result, these de-substantialized instances of economy and power merge into a totality where none of them can gain identity, and the dialectic of the particular (civil society) and the state cannot operate. The "illusory being" of such a system has, however, positive content, but it cannot be understood in the language of the premises on which it was built. In fact, what was called "socialism" was precisely that lame materialization of those premises. "The history of the system," writes Staniszkis, is a constant struggle with the results of that reality, with a stubborn refusal of acceptance by the power that understanding reality on the grounds of its premises is impossible" (1987, p. 61; my translation)

As Staniszkis observes, such a "stubborn refusal" to know is understandable on the part of the people in power – acknowledging that socialism is "illusory being" which needs another identification, would deprive their power of legitimacy. "On the other hand, the refusal to know means that those in power lack factual agency" (p. 61).

Staniszkis's interpretation reveals an important aspect of that political logic which, in my understanding, is a very important feature of relations between educational theory and the political. I have called it epistemology of evasion (Szkudlarek 2014). The "stubborn refusal" to accept the fact that the society "is not what it is" in its conceptual logic *maintains the apparent* in its actual condition of incomprehensible reality. Coming back to the notion of educating society, it was – in its material shape incarnated by the 1970s reforms in Poland – impossible to be understood *as* educating society. It was "something else," but it was too short-lived to be identified by another name or to be described in a different logic. However, as I assume, some of its features can be recognized in the contemporary discourse of learning or the knowledge-based society. In spite of economic, ideological, and technological incompatibilities, both these formations share the feature of being *politically proclaimed* as desirable, and transformed into complex pedagogical regimes, trying to expand the domain of education beyond the walls of the school. This issue is taken up in the following chapter.

Notes

1   This innovative outline of the sociology of education by Znaniecki was never translated into English. Probably the richest account on his educational ideas is accessible in the English language as a collection of his reports written in the 1930s, during his work on the Committee on Education and Social Change at Colombia University, edited by Elżbieta Hałas (Znaniecki 1998). From my perspective, Znaniecki's polemic with Dewey is especially interesting. As Hałas writes in the introduction to this collection, Znaniecki "counterbalanced Dewey's idea of a spontaneous, selective adaptation to the ever-changing present, with controlled self-education for the future created by oneself" (in Znaniecki 1998, p. 24).

2   The name of the author of the introduction is not given in the book. This may indicate the possibility that the original introduction could have been withheld by censors. The book was printed three years after the declaration of the martial law following the Solidarity revolution in 1980, and there is not a single reference to this event in the book.

References

BAUDRILLARD, J. (1983). The Ecstasy of Communication. In FOSTER, H. (ed.) *The Anti-Aesthetic*. Washington, DC: Bay Press.

DELEUZE, G. and GUATTARI, F. (2004). *Anti-Oedipus. Capitalism and Schizophrenia*. London and New York: Continuum.

DEWEY, J. (2001). *Democracy and Education*. [Online] The Pennsylvania State University, Electronic Classics Series. Available from: http://www.naturalthinker.net/trl/texts/Dewey, John/Dewey,_John_-_Democracy_And_Education.pdf. [Accessed: 10th December 2015].

FUKUYAMA, F. (1992). *The End of History and the Last Man*. New York: The Free Press.

GIDDENS, A. (1991). *Modernity and Self-Identity. Self and Society in the Late Modern Age*. Stanford: Stanford University Press.

HEGEL, G.F.W. (2010). *The Science of Logic*. Cambridge: Cambridge University Press.

KOMITET EKSPERTÓW DLA OPRACOWANIA RAPORTU O STANIE OŚWIATY W PRL (1973). *Raport o stanie oświaty w PRL*. Warszawa: Państwowe Wydawnictwo Naukowe.

LACLAU, E. (2005). *On Populist Reason*. London: Verso.

MARX, K. (1845). *Theses on Feuerbach*. [Online] Montclaire State Univeristy. Available from: https://msuweb.montclair.edu/~furrg/gned/marxtonf45.pdf. [Accessed: 10th December 2015].

MEAD, G.H. (1934). *Mind, Self, and Society from the Standpoint of a Social Behaviorist*. Chicago: University of Chicago Press.

PARSONS, T. (1951). *The Social System*. London: Routledge and Kegan Paul.

SICIŃSKI, A. (1983). Społeczeństwo istniejące a pożądane. In SUCHODOLSKI, B. (ed.) *Społeczeństwo wychowujące: rzeczywistość i perspektywy: materiały sesji naukowej*. Wrocław, Warszawa, Kraków, Gdańsk and Łódź: Zakład Narodowy im. Ossolińskich.

STANISZKIS, J. (1987). Ontologia realnego socjalizmu (pierwsze przybliżenie). *Krytyka. Kwartalnik Polityczny*, 26.

STANISZKIS, J. (1992). *The Ontology of Socialism*. Oxford: Clarendon Press.

STRZELECKI, J. (1983), Uwagi o stanie i statusie symboli naczelnych "społeczeństwa wychowującego". In SUCHODOLSKI, B. (ed.) *Społeczeństwo wychowujące: rzeczywistość i perspektywy: materiały sesji naukowej*. Wrocław, Warszawa, Kraków, Gdańsk and Łódź: Zakład Narodowy im. Ossolińskich.

SUCHODOLSKI, B. (ed.) (1983). *Społeczeństwo wychowujące: rzeczywistość i perspektywy: materiały sesji naukowej*. Wrocław, Warszawa, Kraków, Gdańsk and Łódź: Zakład Narodowy im. Ossolińskich.

SZCZEPAŃSKI, J. (1975). *Rzecz o nauczycielach w wychowującym społeczeństwie socjalistycznym*. Warszawa: PIW.

SZKUDLAREK, T. (2014). The Excess of Theory. On the Functions of Educational Theory in Aapparent Reality. In BIESTA, G., ALLAN, J. and EDWARDS, R. (eds.) *Making a Difference in Theory. The Theory Question in Education and the Education Question in Theory*. London and New York: Routledge.

WOŁCZYK, J. (1974). *Elementy polityki oświatowej*. Warszawa: PWN.

ŽIŽEK, S. (1989). *The Sublime Object of Ideology*. London: Verso.

ZNANIECKI, F. (1973). *Socjologia wychowania*. Warszawa: Państwowe Wydawnictwo Naukowe.

ZNANIECKI, F. (1998). *Education and Social Change*. Frankfurt am Mein, Berlin, Bern, New York, Paris and Wien: Peter Lang.

Chapter 5

Knowledge, education, and ignorance

In this chapter, I address the relations between educational thought and the political construction of society in neoliberal discourse and, in particular, in the concept of the knowledge-based society (KBS) which it has spawned. This discursive space is not an educational theory in the proper sense. Although it originated in the debate on economic reforms, it profoundly structured the field of educational thinking, and, indeed, it operates from the position traditionally occupied by theories of education. Before I address this issue, let me recall, as the point of departure, some features identified thus far that pertain to educational theories.

In educational theories analyzed in the previous chapters, the connection between pedagogical and political forms of modern government appear to be bi-directional. Education is meant to create autonomous citizens capable of articulating a social contract (as in Rousseau) and who are equipped with strong moral characters (as in Herbart), both of which are necessary in a republican society; simultaneously, such a society is gradually conceptualized in way that makes it both a subject (agent) and a possible object of pedagogical interventions. The case of socialist pedagogy in Poland illustrates this possibility very well. In other words, while education is identified in political terms, politics is, thus, grounded in education. This retroactive movement, reflecting the gesture of "grounding the foundation" in Hegel (1873), is seen by F. Tony Carusi (2011, see further) as typical of metaphorization. Within this broad metaphoric articulation, there are yet three more specific instances of such connections. The first is Rousseau's educational naturalism, where human nature reveals itself owing to the work of political institutions which must be established according to that nature. The second is Herbart's mechanicism, which pushed the "hydrologies" of fluid discipline outside educational mechanics, and created conditions for attributing the agency and responsibility for dispersed disciplinary practices to the construct of "society," or the state. The third is the discourse of educating society which treated such dispersed practices of power, conditioning the possibilities of education, as targets of pedagogical control themselves. On the one hand, such metaphors *identify* education as something non-educational (as supplementing nature, as mental mechanics, as a socialist society); on the other, they *grounded* these non-educational phenomena in education (the nature of Rousseau's nation has to be pedagogically revealed or construed; Herbart's mind works properly when supplied with pedagogically controlled aesthetic revelations; socialist Poland is only possible if purposeful education encompasses the totality of social life). In fact, it is not easy to determine which of the elements in such couplings was the first to identify the other. Such bi-directional analysis of the work of metaphor follows F. Tony Carusi's (2011) notion, which I find very productive in the analyses undertaken here, of *coupling* rather than *substitution* being the *modus operandi* of metaphor. Expanding the meaning of metaphor applied in Laclau's work, borrowed from Jacobson and Lacan, where the operation of metaphor is reduced to that of substitution, Carusi develops a copular understanding of metaphor, where the relation between its elements (the tenor and the vehicle) is bi-directional and is that of *identification* and *grounding*. As Carusi says, referring to the operation of the neoliberal discourse of education in the USA,

> [a] substitutive theory of metaphor would claim that the vehicle substitutes for the tenor. As such, a substitutive analysis reads *public education is a market* . . . as a metaphor wherein a market substitutes for public education. However, by isolating of the operations of identification and grounding metaphor elicits a different emphasis. . . . *[P]ublic education is a market* both identifies neoliberal discourse with public education, thus making them indistinguishable, and reaffirms this identity by grounding public education in neoliberal discourse through the deployment of a number of floating signifiers, e.g., competition and accountability. These floating signifiers then retroactively justify the identification of public education with neoliberal discourse resulting in a circular logic that justifies the neoliberalization of education reform. Thus, the copular metaphor at the level of discourse, or discursive metaphor, proves its identification of the vehicle and tenor through the grounding that proceeds from the identification in the first place.
>
> (Carusi 2011, p. 72)

The mutual entanglement of education and politics, identified in previous chapters as structured as metaphor, where both these elements are linked in the operations of identification and grounding, is, thus, transformed smoothly into the relation between education and economy. The substitution of economy for politics is not accidental here, for it is economy that has been raised to the position of universality in the contemporary landscape of power games. Economy is both the reason and the means of social life, and its logic (but not its efficiency) is represented as independent of any other instances of the social. In fact, politics, nowadays often referred to as "post-politics," is seen as functional in relation to economy, which – to use Slavoj Žižek's phrase – is positioned as a "determination of the last instance." (Žižek 2008).

The metaphoric coupling mentioned above means that education is identified in economic terms and economy is rendered dependent on education. This articulation, contrary do the dominant narrative of educational researchers, seems to start with expressing *economy* as relying on education, which retroactively grounds education in the domain of economy. In most educational analyses, we tend to focus on the latter move, seeing it as a nearly intentional colonization of education by the conceptual apparatus of economy. From my perspective, such colonization is rather a secondary phenomenon that is not necessarily intended by the proponents of neoliberal economies: apparently, it is a mere consequence of recognizing their dependence of economy on extra-economic (cultural and educational) factors. Before I address this mutual relation, let us consider the issue of discursive colonization.

The act of colonization is, in a broad sense, an act of social change, an attempt at transforming borders, identities, policies, and cultural practices. It always involves the transformation of meanings; therefore, it is always *discourse* colonization. As Shirley Leitch and Juliet Roper say, its purpose is "to transform both the discourse practices and the broader socio-cultural practices associated with the colonized domains," so that "the new ways of speaking become accepted as 'commonsense'" (1998, p. 204). The construction of commonsense creates the conditions for changing social practices: "if education is perceived to be a business then it is natural to apply the language of business to the classroom" (p. 204). This transformation is a good illustration of the role of metaphor ("education is business") and catachresis (its becoming commonsense) as constitutive of social change, in terms of Laclau's theory (see Chapter 6). Robert Young describes this process in similar terms. "Commerce, by reducing everything in a society to a system of universal equivalency, to a value measured in terms of something else, thus performs an operation of cultural decoding that works according to the linguistic form of metaphor" (Young 2006, p. 164). Such a process is bound to be gradual; it has to be mediated by series of equivalences (according to Umberto Eco, metaphor is a short circuit in the chain of metonymies; [Eco 1984]), and, following Carusi (2011), is bi-directional; metaphor works as *coupling* rather that as one-directional substitution. As Young argues, colonization is never a one-directional process; no culture remains the same when it enters foreign territory. "A culture never repeats itself perfectly away from home. Any exported culture will in some way run amok, go phut or threaten to go mumbo-jumbo as it dissolves in the heterogeneity of the elsewhere" (2006, p. 165). Bi-directionality, or the moment of grounding and identification, will inevitably hybridize or create a "thirdness" between the original terms. Metaphors always address the in-between.[1]

Since the 1980s, the discourse of education, along with that of social work, health, urban development, etc., has been invested (or infested, as many educationalists love to think of it) with economic concepts and ideas. Such investments started not with redefining education, but with the question of non-economic factors of economic growth. The theoretical career of the notion of human capital, as Lily Kong (2000) observes, results from the discovery of the role cultural factors play in economic development. This way of thinking starts with attempts at explaining cases of market failure by information deficits, which, in turn, have to be related to the sphere of communication (Fine and Green 2000). In other words, in highly competitive economies, what "counts" is not only material factors of production, but also social, cultural, and individual factors of attitudes, needs, fears, and desires, etc., and the abilities of market actors to recognize and utilize them.

In this context, the moment of expressing education in economic terms is a secondary, retroactive act of grounding. As A.J. Scott puts it (1997, quoted in Kong 2000), contemporary capitalism arrives at the point where meaning becomes a crucial element of production strategies, *and* (my emphasis) culture as such becomes a commodity. Scott thus points to metonymic contiguity. However, in the neoliberal discourse, such contiguity is expressed like a causal relation and it solidifies as justification strategy: culture is important for economy; *therefore*, it becomes commodified; consequently, it *should* be run like business. Metonymy builds horizontal connections from which new metaphors can be made, and these, in turn, work to "alter the systems of thought," inviting dense conceptual structures of New Public Management. However, the argument that pervades in neoliberal discourse oversteps such a metonymy-metaphor-concept transformation and simply holds that because education is important for economy, schools should be run like businesses (cf. Colclough 1996; Finkelstein and Grubb 2000; Whitty 1997). Logically, it is easy to state that the latter by no means results from the former; psychologically, it is not so. The metaphoric grounding that operates here manages to re-create the whole area of educational imaginary so that we start looking for (and eventually we find) experiential, empirical referents to such theoretical claims, which crystallizes metaphors as quasi-concepts. According to Eco (1984), when metaphors are often used (or abused), they become catachresis; they operate like concepts (e.g., they point to specific referents, like "a leg of the table") and become part of the cultural code. The notions like "school is a service," and "education is a market" (Carusi 2011) become part of common sense, and their contingency becomes invisible.

Technically, the career of economic explanations of the whole area of social behavior relates, according to Fine and Green, to the success of "methodological individualism," that is to the invention of theoretical models that can explain the social as a result of individual choices, rather than the other way around. In this context, models including complex, diversified social factors that are difficult to measure in terms of their importance in overcoming information shortages in the market, have little chance of becoming part of the mainstream economy. Instead, they colonize the areas of other (weaker?) social sciences: "Tell us what non-economic factors you think are important to the economy and how they reflect or create market imperfections. We will then model them on the basis of our own methodology and return them to you as a contribution to your own discipline" mocks the stance of the "cultural capitalists" (Fine and Green 2000, p. 85).

The radical reforms of the Reagan–Thatcher era, which were meant to increase the productivity and competitiveness of Western economies, entailed vast reductions in public spending with simultaneous claims of increasing the efficiency of public "services." Such contradictory aims could be striven for only by means of the overt or hidden and partial or gradual privatization of such services. Not only did New Public Management require radical changes in financial policies, but also in the whole mental framework concerning such issues as individuality, community, responsibility, poverty, prosperity, health, development, civil society, or the State as such. The conceptual structure allowing for such redefinitions was prepared by the aforementioned "discovery of culture" as a factor of economic growth. Thus, social theory has been de-territorialized ("decoded") and re-territorialized as the domain of economic rationality, its key concepts being transcribed into a new jargon opening links to as yet alien discursive territories.[2] Education was identified with human resources management, the forgotten concept of *Bildung* was identified with human capital, and morality – technically seen as social cohesion, mutual bonds, and obligations – with social capital. As these concepts speak to non-educational expertise, the centers of educational thinking, especially when that thinking is meant to direct systemic reforms, moved from faculties of education to those of economics and management, if not to banks directly. The success of this transfer builds on the fact that economic discourse is sufficiently complex to reproduce the basic structures of educational theory. The relations between human and social capital, and the debate between the proponents of effective investments in each of these, play a game known from classic educational debates – that between the proponents of individualism (or psychologism, or liberalism) and collectivism (or sociologism, or communitarianism) in education. The fact that economists claim to be able to calculate long-term and short-term returns from such contrastive investments (Gradstein 2000; Gradstein and Justman 2000) not only makes their discourse rhetorically more compelling than that proposed by educationalists and philosophers, but it allows them to remain comfortably ignorant of their "pre-scientific" considerations. Economy discussing education smoothly and easily emancipates itself from the "science of education."

The ease with which such colonization operates on the body of educational thinking is itself an interesting issue. On the one hand, it may profit from the similarity between "methodological individualism" to the construction of psychology, which is a very powerful associate of educational thinking. On the other, as I suggested elsewhere, it may be linked to the self-effacing weakness of educational theory, often marginalized and kept quiet in public debates. When pedagogical concepts (like *learning* or *assessment*) are re-inscribed and incorporated into the discourse of a Nobel-prize-eligible discipline, situated close to institutions of "real" power, educational researchers may feel *ennobled*. "Didn't we tell you? Education matters!" In other words, what we experience nowadays as colonization may have started with the *fascination* of educational communities with the fact that their "infantile" field of studies had been recognized as important for what "really counts" – for business and economy (Szkudlarek 2001). As Eco (1984) says, successful metaphors work through excitation.

Let us examine how these relations operate within the terrain of knowledge and learning. My thesis is that this terrain is delineated by the instance of ignorance.

Knowledge-based society and the construction of ignorance[3]

The vision of the knowledge-based society (KBS) is not clear. It connects vague concepts and metaphors that form an ideological structure which implies that the knowledge-based economy (KBE) builds (and needs) a knowledge society composed of life-long learning individuals as well as of learning communities and organizations; that people's knowledge and skills are valuable assets in such societies; and that the best way of providing for economic growth and social welfare is investing in their learning. Thus, it is hoped that the human capital created will deliver a relatively quick, supposedly certain return. As I mentioned before, the idea of human capital investment, as guided by the logic of competition, is balanced by that of investments in social capital; therefore, it is not only individuals, but also their communities, families, and cultures that need investment, that learn, and that therefore "count." In general, the links between knowledge, politics, and economy are inevitably mediated by education, usually re-labeled as learning. As Gert Biesta observes, this very label of learning "allows for a re-description of the process of education in terms of an economic transaction" (Biesta 2005, p. 58).

The notion of learning, apart from metaphorizing education as a market transaction, empowers individual subjects and ultimately makes them responsible not only for their narrowly understood learning, but for their meaningful, socially adequate lives in general. This dimension of contemporary education is usually analyzed in terms of Foucault's idea of governmentality (Foucault 1979). As Maarten Simons and Jan Masschelein note, quoting Colin Gordon, the governmentalization of learning and "the assemblage of the learning apparatus" link the grammars of education, social order, and governance. As they say, "[t]his is more than governmentalization of education in its institutional shape: the new regime addresses learning as personal experience. Individuals should be managers of their own learning" (Simons and Masschelein 2008, p. 407). Learning thus becomes not only a force mediating between economy and politics, but the core of the whole apparatus of governnmentality. It is at the same time conceptualized as if it were detached from external determinations – from "the state, from institutions, from the dominance of the teacher, from the impact of economy" (p. 414) – and as if seamlessly integrated with the individual person. We may add that this usually means learning *skills* to do things (which reside "within" a person) rather than (external) things themselves (e.g., we are made to learn "skills to produce knowledge" rather than knowledge itself – see further in this chapter). The project of learning thus contributes to turning individuals into disconnected, monadic "objects": immanent, self-interested, self-sustainable, movable assets of the neoliberal economy.

Apart from being productive of such human objects, the discourse of learning has its socially conscious, more spiritual, utopian dimension. This dimension is present, for instance, in such globally circulated documents as the famous UNESCO report called *Learning: the treasure within*, written under the guidance of Jacques Delors (Delors et al. 1996). The authors of this text, translated into over 30 languages, speak about education as "the necessary utopia" believed capable of resolving tensions between the global and the local, the universal and the individual, between tradition and modernity, long-term and short-term considerations, competition and equality of opportunities, between the expansion of knowledge and the limited capacities of its being absorbed by individuals, and, finally, between the material and the spiritual. This range of issues (or demands, in the language of Laclau's theory) is close to totality. Fully aware of the pressure of economy and of the practical expectations educational audiences have of schools, the authors stress the social, the existential, and the ethical as remedies for the risks and damages brought by the rapid increase in knowledge production, globalization, and economic uncertainty. They speak of four pillars of education: learning *to know*, learning *to do*, learning *to live together/with others*, and learning *to be*. Yet, in spite of this holistic and humanistic attitude, their report – on the rhetorical level, transmitted by the very title of the book and the somewhat heavy metaphor on which it is based – subscribes to the economic rationality which it hopes to transcend:

> For the title of [this] report, the Commission turned to one of La Fontaine's fables, *The Ploughman and his Children:*
>
>> Be sure (the ploughman said), not to sell the inheritance
>> Our forebears left to us
>> A treasure lies concealed therein
>> Readapting slightly the words of the poet, who was lauding the virtues
>>   of hard work, and referring instead to education – that is, to every-
>>   thing that humanity has learned about itself – we could have him say:
>> But the old man was wise
>> To show them before he died
>> *That learning is the treasure.*
>
> (Delors et al. 1996, p. 35)

Not only does the title refer to the ultimate dream of economy (treasure!), but the transformation of the treasure in the excerpt cited strictly reflects the transformations of capital in modern societies as well:

> In the past, it was usually a unique combination of land, labor, and capital that gave a nation its "comparative advantage." Today, things are different. As an ever-increasing percentage of economic growth arises from

the burgeoning knowledge sector, a nation's comparative advantage comes instead from its collective ability to leverage what its citizens know.

(Neef 2009, p. 5)

La Fontaine's ploughman's economy is that of land, labor, and capital (treasure) buried "within" the land. These were the factors of production in the classic economy. Delors's economy is a knowledge economy. Neef's reference to the "collective ability to leverage what . . . citizens know" almost perfectly corresponds to the report's notion of learning. Delors and his colleagues hope that learning/knowledge will lead from economic growth to human development (the title of Chapter 3 of the report), as well as to a world society (through local communities) and democratic participation (through social cohesion). But will it?

As I said, the neoliberal economy invests in human capital and at the same time curbs the costs of such investments. Speaking of humanistic goals of education (learning to live together, to be, etc.) and using economic metaphors as their justification overshadows antagonisms and contradictions between the all-inclusive ideal of learning for everyone and the capitalist economy based on competition and structural inequality. In this context, the "treasure of learning" may contribute to obliterating global tensions and conflictual demands by virtue of being a vague concept which allows for integrating disparate and conflictual demands. I am referring here to the notion of the empty signifier, which, in Laclau's theory (2005; 2014), denotes a catachresis capable of representing incommensurable demands.

Bob Jessop (2008) is helpful in bridging the issue of conflicts and exclusions typical of the logic of capital with the rhetoric of the knowledge society. Referring to Michael Peters, he speaks of "twin concepts" – dual expressions which, one may say, still bear the structure of their metaphorical nature – which arrange the operation of this discourse. The "knowledge economy," the "knowledge worker," and the "knowledge society" are notions (or "dead metaphors") which transform not only the meanings of economy, work, and society, but – along the logic of identification and grounding (Carusi 2011) – redefine knowledge as well. The twin-concept of the knowledge society appears to be, in this account, "a performative ideology with constitutive effects at the level of public policy" (Peters 2006, p. 1; cited in Jessop 2008, p. 20). In terms of Laclau's theory, it is an empty signifier. Its performative role is to integrate disparate demands and, thus, to create an imaginary horizon of social totality.

One may find traces of the creation of this empty signifier in European Union research policy documents. The call for proposals in the EU's Sixth Framework Programme comprised the following description of research objectives:

Research Area 1: Improving the generation, distribution and use of knowledge and its impact on economic and social development.
Research Area 2: Options and choices for the development of a knowledge-based society.
Research Area 3: The variety of paths towards a knowledge society

In another part of the same call we read:

1.1.1 Understanding knowledge

The objective is to integrate research capacities in relation to the economic, social, cultural and cognitive aspects of knowledge, and to the ways in which it functions in the economy, society and polity *in order to place conceptions of "knowledge society" on solid underpinnings*
(European Commission 2005, p. 4; emphasis added)

In other words, we need to research the options and choices for the development of a knowledge society and the variety of paths leading to such a society, but we have no "solid underpinnings" to understand what a knowledge society is. The same agenda commissions research on mapping the roads and paths leading to a clearly named destination, and on specifying what destination there is behind that name.

Along with its role in the construction of contemporary political identities, the discourse of the knowledge society hides behind its elevated rhetoric the divisions and exclusions which build "really existing" knowledge societies. Every social structure is built of differences. The construction of the knowledge society depends not only on the lines of knowledge production, innovation, and learning, but also on the lines of knowledge exclusions. Knowledge can be defined only in relation to the lack of knowledge, to *ignorance* as its "constitutive outside" in Laclau's (2005) terms, as that which defines its limits and marks its territories. Such constitutive exclusions are obliterated by the all-inclusive utopia of learning and the knowledge society, paradoxically expressed in terms of capital. In other words, humanistic discourse – here represented by Jacques Delors's report – obliterates such exclusions and subsumes the structure of knowledge inequalities, produced as such in the course of turning knowledge into capital, into the all-inclusive utopia of global learning for global development.

The capitalization of academic knowledge affects academic institutions in numerous ways, but its most general impact can be described as undercutting the classic idea of the unity between research and education. In a research project run in four European universities (Dahlgren et al. 2007), several aspects of such separation were identified. One illustration is a case reported by a student from Poland. A part-time academic teacher, a psychologist who also worked for a private consultancy company, interrupted her presentation during class to announce that she could not give the students more details because that would constitute selling her knowledge too cheaply. Instead, she invited them to her private company. The interview from which this information was obtained was conducted in 2003, when such cases were rare, and it provoked indignation on the part of the students. In 2015, the same university changed the employment rules for its research staff, and all contracts were supplemented with clauses that advise employees to refrain from publishing research results or including them in course content if they are of potential commercial value until a specific unit of the university estimates potential profits. The Information Security Policy of the same university includes the following regulations:

- *The Rule of Necessary Privilege*: Every employee is granted access to the resources of the University . . . limited to only those resources that are indispensable for the realization of her or his duties
- *The Rule of Justified Knowledge*: Employees have knowledge of the resources of the University . . . limited to the knowledge of issues indispensable for the performance of their duties (Own research. Source of the data anonymized)

Clearly, such regulations make the idea of collegiality in managing an autonomous university, as well as that of the unity between research and education as defining what the university is, strikingly inadequate.

One of the hypothetical interpretations of such cases is that we are witnessing a shift in what can be called "institutional pacts" linking universities with their social milieus (European Commission 2005). While the "classic" (Humboldtian) university could be seen as implicated in the construction of republican societies and national cultures, the emerging pact would be split into two different traits mediated by two separate "products" of academic work. The first pact would link the university to industry on the corporate side, and it is mediated by *knowledge* production. The second pact would link the university to industry on the labor side, and this one is mediated by *skills* production.

This separation seems to be supported by more and more evidence nowadays, and its theoretical conceptualization can be found in Marxist and post-Marxist approaches to the knowledge economy. The classic account on the emergence of capitalist economy assumes that there were two necessary conditions to be met: the production of capital, and the production of the working class (Marx 1887). The latter was based on the enclosures of common land and the eviction of "commoners," so that they had no legal means of survival other than wage employment. The worker is, in this perspective, a person who has nothing but his/her hands to sell. It is often claimed that the current transformation of knowledge into capital involves a similar movement (e.g., Jessop 2007; Philips 2005). The massification of higher education is aimed at the production of knowledge workers who do not have to be equipped with specific knowledge, nor are they expected to have it by their employers. If today's economy is driven by knowledge *production*, its possession cannot be expected of workers. What is needed instead is that they have the *skills* necessary for such production (Szkudlarek 2010).

In this respect, the knowledge economy and its correlate knowledge society emerge within a logic similar to that which guided the emergence of earlier forms of capital. The fact that the persons engaged in knowledge work often resist treating knowledge as a commodity does not seem to hamper this

development. As Bob Jessop argues in his paper on Karl Polanyi's contribution
to the theory of capital, knowledge *is* a fictitious commodity, but the case with
land, labor, and money was exactly the same:

> One of Polanyi's most important contributions to critical social science
> was his insistence that land, labour, and money were fictitious commodities
> and that the liberal propensity to treat them as if they were real commodi-
> ties was a major source of contradictions and crisis-tendencies in capitalist
> development – so great that society would eventually fight back against the
> environmentally and socially destructive effects of such treatment.
>
> (Jessop 2007, p. 115)

Jessop describes the commodification of knowledge as following the same stages
as those that were identified in the process of turning land, labor, and money
into the factors of production in earlier phases of capitalism. In this context, the
current tendencies, on the one hand, to subordinate knowledge to measurable
"impact factors," to integrate it into the flow of monetary capital (knowledge-
technology transfer policies), to expand intellectual property rights regulations,
etc. – and the emergence of the "knowledge commons" movement and its
more mainstream varieties, like open-access publications – present exactly the
same logic as that pertaining to the commodification of earlier forms of assets.
The fictitious commodity of knowledge, treated as if it were a real commodity,
causes destructive effects that are resisted and countered by attempts to reconstruct enclaves of knowledge commons. Both these movements are part of the
same political logic of knowledge capitalism, and they clearly repeat earlier
developments of the system. To refer to the case of a university introducing
strict regulations as to the use of research results that potentially can be com-
mercialized, one should note that in the same country there are binding regulations concerning open-access publication of research results that are obtained
using public monies. Researchers are obliged to immediately make their results
accessible in open repositories; this accurately illustrates Jessop's observation of
the system trying to "repair damages" it has made or to prevent them. However, the same regulation reminds researchers that they must not disobey the
rules of research commercialization. On the other hand, open-access publishing
can itself be understood as supportive of commercialization and, for instance,
similar to advertising campaigns.[4] These apparently colliding ideologies, representing conflictual forces of capital and democracy operating within the same
state, have to be resolved independently in every respective case and by every
researcher herself; thus, they become a pedagogy that makes every employee
constantly *think* of herself as implicated in the conflicting roles of the university
and personally responsible for the ways she embodies them. In other words,
the collision between the public mission of the university and its implication
in the capitalist knowledge economy, which cannot be resolved in a stable way
by political means, is pushed down to the level of individual responsibility, and

it is individuals who have to learn how to act within the space delineated by conflicting normative orders.

Jessop's conception of economic imaginaries (Jessop 2008) gives more substance to how such fictitious constructions as "human capital" or the "knowledge economy" operate as performative agents and how they gradually change into solid material realities. The idea of the knowledge-based economy, invented and actively promoted by the OECD (OECD 1996), organized numerous elements of the public discourse, standardized the language, and gradually created a hegemonic complex of imaginaries through which social realities have been understood and transformed.

> The rise of KBE as the hegemonic economic imaginary was neither a fateful necessity nor an arbitrary act of will. It resulted from the operation of the usual evolutionary mechanism of variation, selection, and retention as the social forces backing one or another economic imaginary compete for support in a particular, complex conjuncture.
>
> (Jessop 2008, p. 28)

In this context, the split between skills education and knowledge education, the tension between the public and the commercial distribution of knowledge, and the restricted access to knowing within academic institutions should be read as a condition of the construction of knowledge capitalism. In other words, we are speaking here of the *production, distribution, and management of unknowing*, of *ignorance* as the border of knowledge enclosures and as the point of reference in measuring the *value* of knowledge capital.

Until recently, such a statement could easily be criticized as exaggerated or ideologically biased. However, in recent publications, we find direct references to ignorance as a planned and carefully managed aspect of information and knowledge production policies. As Joanne Roberts and John Armitage write,

> the knowledge economy is precisely rooted in the production, distribution, and consumption of ignorance and lack of information. What we are suggesting, then, is that the so-called knowledge economy is one wherein the production and use of knowledge also implies the creation and exploitation of ignorance. For not only knowledge but also ignorance now plays a main role in the formation of advanced global capitalism.
>
> (Roberts and Armitage 2008, p. 345)

One could understand this statement as a fairly typical example of managerial discourse, where what emerges as critical de-masking is re-appropriated as a problem to be managed and included in rational policy making. In other words, the functioning of a knowledge society and a knowledge economy requires making particular persons ignorant about things that concern them in order to do business or implement a policy. Robert Proctor and Londa Schiebinger (2008) propose in this context a program for *agnotology* – a systematic study in ignorance. In the Introduction to their volume, Proctor says: "We need to think about the conscious, unconscious, and structural production of ignorance, its diverse causes and conformations, whether brought about by neglect, forgetfulness, myopia, extinction, secrecy, or suppression. The point is to question the naturalness of ignorance, its causes and its distribution" (Proctor and Scheibinger 2008, p. 3).

Knowledge society: Ontology and ethics

The relations between education and politics in the discourse of the knowledge-based society can be interpreted through the two ontological perspectives already presented in this book. The first is the one introduced in Chapter 4, where I discuss the idea of "educating society" developed in the 1970s in socialist Poland. In that case, education was identified with the construction of a socialist society, while such a society was retroactively grounded in "total" education permeating all social institutions and coordinated and monitored by schools. In some practical aspects, this role of the school was not far from current expectations concerning life-long learning, recognition of prior learning, etc., with the fundamental difference that the former Polish regime aimed at social attitudes, while skills are the focus nowadays. The ground for such similarity is, apart from the somewhat total approach to managing education and society, the top-down strategy of implementation. Both these ideologies were invented as certain imaginary horizons by political elites concerned with structural crises or deficits (the lack of political legitimacy for the project of state socialism in 1970s Poland, and the insufficient knowledge capital for a competitive global economy nowadays), and both had to be translated into material forces capable of changing respective social structures. The inclusive utopianism of both of these discourses helps to legitimize their more or less coercive character, on the one hand, and to obliterate exclusions and inequalities necessary for and resulting from their implementation, on the other. In this context, the results of policies organized by the ideologies of KBE and KBS, along with their overarching neoliberal doctrine, seem to fall into the same trap which Jadwiga Staniszkis (1992) identified in the projects of Polish socialism. Both policies are based on abstract conceptual models focused on "essences" rather than on complex descriptions of heterogeneous and overdetermined realities, even though the Open Coordination Method invented in Europe as a means for the implementation of KBS was meant to be sensitive to specific contexts and particularities (cf. Robertson 2008). However, that very method demanded that comparable, and, thus, universalized and coercive, *measures* had to be invented so that the task of coordination could be possible at all. The intended openness quickly collapsed under the weight of the coordination instruments.

Reviving Hegel's dialectic of reality and appearance, Staniszkis reminds that political actions guided by conceptual assumptions must produce *apparent realities*. Whatever policy we make of conceptual blueprints, it is incomprehensible in terms of these blueprints; it cannot be understood as their incarnation. Whatever solidifies into material reality is an incarnation not only of its essential, conceptually representable premises, but also of infinite interactions between accidental features and unpredictable effects of such incarnations themselves. The knowledge-based society, apart from being conceptualized *as* fiction (cf. the notion of fictitious capital of knowledge in Jessop 2007), *becomes* fiction when it materializes – it is "absurd" and *incomprehensible* in terms of its founding logic. A knowledge-based society cannot be comprehended as a "knowledge-based" society. Demanding knowledge, it is structured by its limits, exclusions, and dispossessions; by the distribution of simple skills, by the flows and crystallizations of ignorance, and by the uncontrollable growth of institutions and procedures which enforce rigid indices of the value of thus created capital; and by a myriad of factors we will never identify. Other languages need to be invented to describe such a reality. Andrè E. Mazawi (2013) shows how such complex realities, produced by means of the apparently simple and robust policies of privatization and deregulation, escape the logic and structural distinctions (including the distinction between the public and the private) productive of these realities.

The second ontological perspective, complementary to the one described above, is based on Ernesto Laclau's theory (it will be presented in more detail in the following chapter). In spite of rejecting Hegel's logic as a theory of the social, Laclau operates in a similar space. One may say that appearance, which is a result of the dialectic of essence in Hegel, is, under the label of radical heterogeneity, the point of departure for the theory of identity in Laclau. Societies are heterogeneous, and they cannot be subsumed to any conceptual logic, and, thus, they cannot be fully represented. At the same time, they need identity, and their political agency needs some symbolic body. Such identity must therefore be construed by rhetorical means, and a chief role is played here by the dynamics of equivalence (where particular demands are articulated in a chain-like structure opposing an excluded element of the social) and hegemony, which implies that one of these particular demands is "elevated to the dignity of the Thing" (Laclau 2005, numerous occurrences) and invested with the meaning of totality. Such hegemonic signifiers are *empty*, not only in terms of *not* representing anything outside the chain of signifiers (such totality of a fully reconciled and fully representable society does not exist), but in terms of *representing that very lack* as well (Laclau 2005; 2014).

Speaking of the notion of knowledge-based society as an empty signifier means that it originally denoted a *particular* demand (like an economic fantasy of the West being capable of competing with emerging economies without dramatically compromising its own quality of life), and, as such, it was more precisely represented by the label of the knowledge-based economy. Its re-branding into KBS marked the moment of its being invested with demands and expectations concerning other, non-economic spheres of social life, such as education (redefined as learning), individual biographies and governmentality strategies, employment (mutated into employability), social welfare, creativity, the reduction of public debt, high culture, urban design, migration, the empowerment of civil society, privatization, and the like. Articulating such diverse demands, it colonized vast terrains of social imagination, including the hopes and expectations of people engaged in as yet non-commercial activities such as the arts and humanities.[5] The complex of signifiers articulated around KBS (KBE, learning, etc.) was, thus, elevated to the position of the hegemonic, all-encompassing ideal believed capable of resolving all tensions (cf. Delor's report) and integrating all heterogeneous demands and expectations concerning the reconstruction of the social.

The postulational rhetoric, identified in previous chapters as characteristic of educational theory, operates in the discourse of KBS as well. KBS is a desired form of society; it *ought to* come true, and educationalists *ought to* work toward its realization. It works as a value rather than as a descriptive category. Such a postulate overshadows the fact that *any* society is a knowledge-based society, and that knowledge is the indispensable glue of human associations and the indispensable vehicle of force and of the power capable of creating social structures. Working *toward* a knowledge-based society, we, in fact, are working toward *some variety* of a knowledge society, where something counts as knowledge while something else does not. The ideology of KBS transforms the meaning of knowledge and invests the meaning of society into some particular types of knowledge, namely, those that can be capitalized and are of commercial value. In the discursive space of the knowledge-based society, students following their interests in the arts and humanities are expected to excuse themselves; they need to explain their position in the society and to invent arguments that help others understand that their knowledge (if it qualifies as knowledge at all) is also valid.

Performing numerous practical and symbolic functions, education contributes to the creation and petrification of the instances of invisibility which secure the operations of the "apparent" KBS. In this respect, it develops an *epistemology of evasion*, a set of cognitive strategies which permit living in the apparent, which teaches not to question its status, and which delays the moment in which the apparent is recognized *as* apparent, as a contingent, overdetermined reality always incommensurable with its symbolic representations. The invisibility of appearance resulting from the impossibility of its being comprehended in terms of its founding logic is, thus, reaffirmed by education that "stabilizes" such an apparent condition (which Laclau calls "the ontic") as "all there is," as the daily routine of living. At the same time, education is implicated in the production and distribution of ignorance that is masked by the loudly pronounced care for knowledge and in the production of skills in learners who, dispossessed of knowledge, become monadic particles, movable workers employable in knowledge industries.

Pedagogies of ignorance

The final issue is more practical, and, by virtue, an ethical one. What do we do with ignorance? The history of educational thought has undoubtedly circulated around this issue. From Plato's gesture of leading people out of the cave of *doxa*, through the mission of spreading God's word to those who were ignorant of the promise of salvation, through making common people part of the realm of letters, through the Enlightenment, through promoting critical thinking, to the current faith in the knowledge society and in turning people into life-long learners, we have thought of education as aimed against ignorance. The current awareness of exclusions made on the way to knowing brings the question of ignorance back to the fore. Ignorance is still at play, because it has not been eradicated; on the contrary, if knowledge is meant to be *the capital* of the new world, ignorance is a necessary negative force that gives knowledge its value. What I know counts only against the background of what others do not. Obviously, the awareness of ignorance being cultivated for the sake of turning knowledge into capital inspires resistance. With the hope of defending the conditions of republicanism and liberal democracy, we revive the ideal of knowledge for all: creative commons, the right to information relevant to the needs of public government, open access to research results – these are the slogans on the banners of current political struggles and on the agendas of democratic governments, at least when they are reminded of their excessive compliance with the demands of global capital. To sum up, thus, we seem, at first glance, to have three instances of ignorance at play: "natural" ignorance (childish, savage, primitive *doxa*), which we combat on the way to a better (rational, divine, or just) society; *managed* and *distributed* ignorance as the negative background against which the value of knowing is defined and capitalized; and latter ignorance *resisted* by critical thought and critical education.

Somewhere on the margins of this narrative dwells another instance of ignorance: the "holy" ignorance that saves the natural goodness of the child from being spoiled by a corrupt world. Rousseau's idea of negative pedagogy, which clearly refers to theological tradition in this respect, introduces a positive connotation to the pedagogy of ignorance; it constitutes a move which may be seen as foretelling the challenging position taken by Jacques Rancière (1991). Rancière reminds us that when acting with the aim of fighting inequalities, we act on the territory charted by the distribution of such inequalities and are in fact trapped in their endless reproduction. His critique of educational reforms undertaken in the 1970s by the French government inspired by Pierre Bourdieu's theory of the reproduction of inequalities, prepared the ground for his claim that inequalities should be *ignored* rather than fought against. In other words, when acting pedagogically, one should make a radical, counter-factual assumption that *all intelligences are equal*, that everybody can learn everything, and that anybody can teach anything. Paradoxical in a way that is comparable to Rousseau's rhetoric, this claim is meant to break the circle of impossibility and to make us act *as if* everything was possible. Only such a radical assumption permits shifting the borders of "the sensible," and of the ways our worlds are structured by aesthetic regimes of perceptions (Rancière 2010). This perspective is significantly developed for education by Gert Biesta (2005; 2010; 2011), Jan Masschelein and Maarten Simons (2013; 2013a), Carl Anders Säfström (2013), and other thinkers who are searching for ways out of the contemporary standstill in the pedagogical imagination. I will return to this element of Rancière's thought when summarizing the issue of invisibility constructed in educational theories in the last chapter of this book. Here, I would like to transpose this radical approach and suggest that one could consider yet another answer to the question I asked a moment ago. What do we do with the awareness that ignorance is produced, managed, and capitalized in knowledge economies? What can we do about the enforced ignorance implanted into the procedures organizing academic work? Can we simply *ignore* them? Obviously, resistance is a crucial issue here; one needs to expose such cases, discuss them, and care whether academic institutions are reduced to functions dictated by their profit-oriented reformers. However, as long as universities need to be revitalized nowadays, it seems that, to large an extent, they need to be re-invented as well. Ignoring what they are in their present shape and ignoring the impossibilities implanted into their tissues may prove to be the prerequisite of change. The cover of the most recent and the most extensive book devoted to ignorance (Gross and McGoey 2015) displays graffiti that reads: "Not ignorance, but ignorance of ignorance is the death of knowledge." It will be most interesting to wait for Jacques Rancière's comment on this declaration. In my understanding, compelling as it is in its Socratic wisdom, it ignores the possibility of seeing ignorance as a condition of transformative action. Once again, can we *ignore* ignorance imposed on us in the course of turning knowledge into capital? Can we assume that, in spite of what we know about being ignorant, we ignore that knowledge refusing to accept the impossibility of knowing and sharing what we know? Sometimes one does not need to know that one knows of such impossibilities. F. Tony Carusi (personal communication) has called such ignorance a reverse of the Socratic stance: from "all I know is that I know nothing" to "I know nothing of all I know." In Maria Mendel's account (2013), this kind of ignorance is called "the knowledge to refuse."

Notes

1   I have mentioned previously that the movement from identification to grounding resembles that analyzed in Hegel's dialectic of identity. The major difference between that Hegelian tradition and the perspective of postcolonial theory represented by Young (to which I am closer) is in how "the third term" is understood. In Hegel, who speaks of the dialectic of identity in logical terms, the difference is resolved by way of synthesis: the third term is a concept and as such it enters the system of other concepts in logical relations. Postcolonial thinkers challenge this perspective by speaking of the impossibility of *Aufhebung*, of the appropriation of difference by way of synthesis, or generalization.

What results from such dialectics, or collisions, are hybrids (which have the form of metaphors) rather than clear-cut concepts (Young 2004). Nevertheless, such hybrids/metaphors can *work* like concepts when they become "domesticated," or crystallized as elements of what Eco calls "cultural code" (Eco 1984).

2   These geographical concepts were introduced by Deleuze and Guattari in their *Anti-Oedipus*. I am using them in the context of colonization after Robert Young (Young 2006, Chapter 7).

3   The following section uses excerpts of a previously written paper (Szkudlarek and Zamojski, 2016).

4   I owe this comment to F. Tony Carusi (personal communication).

5   One of the protest campaigns organized by people employed in cultural institutions in Poland that were suffering from constant cost reduction reforms was run under the slogan *Culture counts*. It was probably hoped that the message would reach the budgetary decision makers of cultural institutions, but, at the same time, in a suicidal gesture, it fully endorsed the discourse of accountability which lies behind the decisions impoverishing these institutions.

References

BIESTA, G. (2005). Against Learning. Reclaiming a Language for Education in an Age of Learning. *Nordisk Pedagogik*, 25, pp. 54–66.

BIESTA, G. (2010). A New Logic of Emancipation. The Methodology of Jacques Rancière. *Educational Theory*, 60 (1), pp. 39–59.

BIESTA, G. (2011). The Ignorant Citizen: Mouffe, Rancière, and the Subject of Democratic Education. *Studies in Philosophy and Education*, 30, pp. 141–153.

CARUSI, F.A. (2011). *The Persistence of Policy: A Tropological Analysis of Contemporary Education Policy Discourse in the United States*. [Online] Scholar Works. Available from: http://scholarworks.gsu.edu/eps_diss/82/ [Accessed: 29th November 2015].

COLCLOUGH, C. (1996). Education and the Market. Which Parts of the Neoliberal Solution are Correct? *World Development*, 24 (4), pp. 589–610.

DAHLGREN, L-O., HANDAL, G., SZKUDLAREK, T. and BAYER, M. (2007). Students as Journeymen Between Cultures of Higher Education and Work: A Comparative European Project on the Transition from Higher Education to Working Life. *Higher Education in Europe*, 32 (4), pp. 305–316.

DELORS, J. et al. (1996). *Learning: The Treasure within. Report to UNESCO of the International Commission on Education for the Twenty-first Century*. [Online] UNESCO Publishing. Available from: http://unesdoc.unesco.org/images/0010/001095/109590eo.pdf. [Accessed: 10th November 2015].

ECO, U. (1984). *The Role of the Reader: Explorations in the Semiotics of Texts*. Bloomington: Indiana University Press.

EUROPEAN COMMISSION (2005). *EU Research on Social Sciences and Humanities. Students as Journeymen Between Communities of Higher Education and Work. Journeymen Final report*. [Online] European Commission. Available from: http://cordis.europa.eu/documents/documentlibrary/82608291EN6.pdf. [Accessed: 10th December 2015].

FINE, B. and GREEN, F. (2000). Economics, Social Capital and the Colonization of Social Sciences. In BARON, S., FIELD, J. and SCHULLER, T. (eds.) *Social Capital. Critical Perspectives*. Oxford: Oxford University Press.

FINKELSTEIN, N.D. and GRUBB, W.N. (2000). Making Sense of Education and Training Markets: Lessons from England. *American Educational Research Journal*, 37 (3), pp. 589–610.

FOUCAULT, M. (1979). Governmentality. *Ideology and Consciousness*, 6, pp. 5–21.

GRADSTEIN, M. (2000). An Economic Rationale for Public Education: The Value of Commitment. *Journal of Monetary Economics*, 45 (2), pp. 463–474.

GRADSTEIN, M. and JUSTMAN, M. (2000). Human Capital, Social Capital and Public Schooling. *European Economic Review*, 44 (4–6), pp. 879–890.

GROSS, M. and MCGOEY, L. (eds.) (2015). *Routledge International Handbook of Ignorance Studies*. London: Routledge.

HEGEL, G.F.W. (1873). *The Encyclopaedia of the Philosophical Sciences*. [Online] Available from https://www.marxists.org/reference/archive/hegel/works/sl/introduction.pdf. [Accessed: 10th December 2015].

JESSOP, B. (2007). Knowledge as a Fictitious Commodity: Insights and Limits of a Polanyian Analysis. In BUIĞRA, A. and AĞARTAN, K. (eds.) *Reading Karl Polanyi for the 21st Century: Market Economy as a Political Project*. Basingstoke: Palgrave.

JESSOP, B. (2008). A Cultural Political Economy of Competitiveness and its Implications for Higher Education. In JESSOP, B., FAIRCLOUGH, N. and WODAK, R. (eds.) *Education and the Knowledge-based Economy in Europe*. Rotterdam: Sense.

KONG, L. (2000). Culture, Economy, Politics. Trends and Developments. *Geoforum*, 31 (4), pp. 385–390.

LACLAU, E. (2005). *On Populist Reason*. London: Verso.

LACLAU, E. (2014). *The Rhetorical Foundations of Society*. London: Verso.

LEITCH, S. and ROPER, J. (1998). Genre Colonization as a Strategy. A Framework for Research and Practice. *Public Relations Review*, 24 (2), pp. 203–218.

MARX, K. (1887). *Capital: A Critique of Political Economy*. Vol I, Book One. [Online] Available from: https://www.marxists.org/archive/marx/works/1867-c1/. [Accessed: 10th November 2015].

MASSCHELEIN, J. and SIMONS, M. (2013). *In Defence of the School: A Public Issue*. Leuven and Belgium: Education, Culture & Society.

MASSCHELEIN, J. and SIMONS, M. (2013a). The Politics of the University: Movements of (de-)identification and the Invention of Public Pedagogic Forms. In SZKUDLAREK, T. (ed.) *Education and the Political. New Theoretical Articulations*. Rotterdam, Boston and Taipei: Sense Publishers.

MAZAWI, A.E. (2013). Grammars of Privatization, Schooling, and the Network State. In SZKUDLAREK, T. (ed.) *Education and the Political. New Theoretical Articulations*. Rotterdam, Boston and Taipei: Sense Publishers.

MENDEL, M. (2013). Toward the Ignorant Gdańsk Citizen. Place-based Identity, Knowledge to Refuse, and the Refusal to Know. In SZKUDLAREK, T. (ed.) *Education and the Political. New Theoretical Articulations*. Rotterdam, Boston and Taipei: Sense Publishers.

NEEF, D. (2009). Introduction: Re-thinking Economics in the Knowledge-based Economy. In NEEF, D., SIESFIELD, G.A. and CEFOLA, J. (eds.) *The Economic Impact of Knowledge*. Woburn: Butterworth-Heinemann.

OECD, 1996. *The Knowledge-based Economy*. Paris: OECD.

PHILIPS, D. (2005). Economics as Ideological Phantasy: Dispensability of Man by Way of Changing the Nature of Ideas. *International Journal of Applied Semiotics*, 4 (2), pp. 9–34.

PROCTOR, R.N. and SCHIEBINGER, L. (eds.) (2008). *Agnotology: The Making and Unmaking of Ignorance*. Stanford: Stanford University Press.

RANCIÈRE, J. (1991). *The Ignorant Schoolmaster. Five Lessons in Intellectual Emancipation*. Stanford: Stanford University Press.

RANCIÈRE, J. (2010). *Dissensus: On Politics and Aesthetics*. London: Continuum.

ROBERTS, J. and ARMITAGE, J. (2008). The Ignorance Economy. *Prometheus*, 26 (4), pp. 335–354

ROBERTSON, S.L. (2008). Embracing the Global: Crisis and the Creation of New Semiotic Order to Secure Europe's Knowledge-based Economy. In JESSOP, B., FAIRCLOUGH, N. and WODAK, R. (eds.) *Education and the Knowledge-Based Economy in Europe*. Rotterdam and Taipei: Sense Publishers.

SÄFSTRÖM, C.A. (2013). Stop Making Sense. And Hear the Wrong People Speak. In SZKUDLAREK, T. (ed.) *Education and the Political. New Theoretical Articulations*. Rotterdam, Boston and Taipei: Sense Publishers.

SIMONS, M. and MASSCHELEIN, J. (2008). The Governmentalization of Learning and the Assemblage of a Learning Apparatus. *Educational Theory*, 58 (4), pp. 391–415.

STANISZKIS, J. (1992). *The Ontology of Socialism*. Oxford: Clarendon Press.

SZKUDLAREK, T. (2001). Ekonomia i etyka: przemieszczenia dyskursu edukacyjnego. *Teraźniejszość, Człowiek, Edukacja*. Special Issue.

SZKUDLAREK, T. (2010). Inner University, Knowledge Workers and Liminality. In THOMPSON, P. and WALKER, M. (eds.) *The Routledge Doctoral Student's Companion. Getting to Grips with Research in Education and the Social Sciences*. London: Routledge.

SZKUDLAREK, T. and ZAMOJSKI, P. (2016). *Knowledge, Thinking, Ignorance*. In print.

WHITTY, G. (1997). Creating Quasi-Markets in Education. A Review of Recent Research on Parental Choice and School Autonomy in Three Countries. In APPLE, M. (ed.) *Review of Research in Education*. Washington, DC: AERA.

YOUNG, R.J.C. (2004). *White Mythologies. Writing History and the West*. Abingdon and New York: Routledge.

YOUNG, R.J.C. (2006). *Colonial Desire. Hybridity in Theory, Culture and Race*. London and New York: Routledge.

ŽIŽEK, S. (2008). *In Defense of the Lost Causes*. London: Verso.

Chapter 6

Rhetoric, the political, and education, in light of Laclau's theory

My intention throughout this book is to underscore a possibility that theories of education (including the broad, dispersed forms of educational discourses in which they operate nowadays) are implicated in politics, not only as rational projects of implementing specific visions of political order, but also by their implication in the *ontological* dimension of the political, by their role in creating discursive conditions for the very construability of the social under given historical circumstances.

As I announce in Chapter 1, I am reading educational theories as discourses in the Laclauan, ontological understanding of the term. In this chapter, I am presenting a more systematic account of the role of rhetoric in political ontology. Not all the rhetorical aspects of theories analyzed thus far can be explained in Laclau's terms. I will, therefore, supplement his theory with other conceptions which address issues raised by Laclau's critics, as well as those which seem to be important for the implementation of Laclau's thought in educational research. I also point to other connections between his theory and theories of education (not necessarily those discussed in previous chapters). I hope that this discussion will place the idea of the politics of theory on more solid underpinnings, and that the partial analyses presented thus far gain a more systematic shape.

Laclau's ontological rhetoric[1]

According to Ernesto Laclau, society is a radical construction that does not stem from any natural or otherwise ontologically fundamental basis; it does not work according to any predestined rationality. It is radically heterogeneous, its conflicts do not subscribe to any developmental logic, and it must construe itself by way of that which defines its structures, that is, by discursive means. As I have mentioned referring to Kevin Inston (2010, see Chapter 2), this radical approach continues that of J.J. Rousseau. In other words, because of its radical heterogeneity, society appears to be *ontologically impossible*; it can never attain a complete, fully conceivable shape (Laclau 2005). On the other hand, it is *politically necessary*: it has to be striven for, its identity, however precarious, is indispensable as the condition of political agency. "This totality is an object which is both impossible and necessary. Impossible, because the tension between equivalence and difference is ultimately insurmountable; necessary, because without some kind of closure, however precarious it might be, there would be no signification and no identity" (Laclau 2005, p. 70). Discourse is understood here ontologically, as the domain of relations that *precede* the meaning of particular elements. As objectivity relies on relations, discourse is seen as the medium, or the "terrain" of the objectivity of the social (Laclau 2005, p. 68).

These general assumptions allow for linking education and educational theorizing to the domain of the political in a way difficult to attain in other theoretical perspectives. It suffices to note that if we treat theories as discursive formations, and if we look at educational practice from the perspective of its textual, communicative dimensions, education, in its theoretical/practical totality, positions itself *within* the ontological process of the creation of political entities rather than as merely functional to such processes. In other words, apart from being functional to current forms of political power, it contributes to the production of discursive resources necessary for the construction of *any* political entity, for the construction of *the political* understood as the ontological process of creating the frameworks of social life. The aim of this chapter is to give more substance to this assumption by articulating it in the language of Laclau's theory, supplemented by elements necessary for grasping the specificity of education as compared to political practices, which was the theme of Laclau's analyses.

Laclau is radically critical towards theories and ideological positions, right or left, that rely on historical necessity, rational objectivity, economical determination, or any other deterministic presumption. He challenges the idea of politics as a rational system which permits inferences as to objectively grounded political action which could, thus, be claimed to be "necessary." He opposes the Hegelian and Marxist tradition, where social changes follow the objective logic of conflicting ideas (as in Hegel) or conflicting material forces (as in Marx) revealing themselves in history. In both these theories, according to Laclau, their logical coherence can be gained only at the expense of exclusions, i.e., of eliminating, from theoretical models, those elements of the social that are heterogeneous and cannot be subscribed to the logic of the system. For instance, Hegel ignores "peoples without history," and Marx's binary conflict between labor and capital can be theorized only when social heterogeneity is locked under the label of *lumpenproletariat* (Laclau 2005). The problem is not one of Laclau's being "against exclusion"; on the contrary, Laclau criticizes Hegel and Marx for their failure to make exclusion a significant part of their theoretical models, because, as he claims, no identity can be striven for without exclusion, and one of the main tasks of theory is to explain such a relation. Instead of *theorizing* exclusion as constitutive of their logics, Hegel and Marx *perform* it while setting the ground for their theoretical models.

A very important distinction that structures Laclau's theory is that between *the ontic* and *the ontological*. These concepts echo the Heideggerian distinction, in spite of Laclau's ontology being absolutely different from that of Heidegger. The distinction is explained in detail in his book on populism (2005). Laclau observes that, even though populism has been given extensive attention in political debates, there is no agreement as to the nature of this phenomenon. The reason for such a failure is that all previous attempts were based on the search for the specific, *ontic* content of populist ideologies (right-wing orientation, blaming elites for the misfortunes of common people, etc.). Instead, Laclau defines populism in *ontological* terms and speaks of its fundamental role in the political construction of societies. What is ontological here is that no society has a stable or predefined identity, and, thus, that society needs to establish itself in the course of political action, which, in turn, is impossible without populist mobilization. On the ontic level, populism is always "about something" (e.g., anti-elitism, poverty, or immigration). On the ontological level, such particular issues are representations of the on-going and never-ending struggle of those who are deprived of the right to fully participate in social life (*plebs*) and articulate their diverse demands into a political front which claims to represent the whole of society (*populus*). In sum, the ultimate (and impossible) political demand is that of objectivity, identity, or totality (synonyms in Laclau) of a "fully reconciled society" (Laclau 2005). The way I have been referring to this distinction in previous chapters (for instance, while distinguishing between the instances of invisibility in Rousseau), referred to this Laclauian understanding of the ontic and the ontological.

The whole process of construing such "impossible totality" is described by Laclau as that of the production, articulation, and transformation of demands which are the minimal "building blocks" of political ontology. Demands are reactional to particular and always numerous faults, or lacks in social structures. In other words, they emerge in reaction to injustice, unemployment, the lack of equal opportunities, etc. – to numerous experiences pointing to the "incompleteness" of the political organization of society. Laclau insists that they are prior to the existence of social groups whose identities are built around them, somewhat like in psychoanalysis, where individual subjectivity emerges from the desire of fullness following, for example, separation from the mother's breast. Such identities follow a more general demand – that of being a whole, fully reconciled society. As much as particular demands follow specific faults of the social system, making such a system "incomplete," that very incompleteness results in a generalized demand of social identity, or totality (Laclau 2005). Analogically to the psychoanalytical example, that demand is never to be fulfilled (society will never become complete), although it must be fought for, because societies cannot act collectively without acquiring some identity, without a shared representation of their agency, however precarious that may be.

The crucial element of Laclau's theory relates to the question of how such identity is construed. Social demands are diverse and always particular, and identity requires some universality. Such a universal dimension can be attained only when conceptually incommensurable demands, representing numerous faults in the social system, are articulated against a particular location in the social structure which is seen as blocking the constitution of totality: to "the other." Such a relation to otherness is indispensable, because there are no *logical* ways to move from particular demands, which represent separate aspects of social reality, or faults of separate policies (like unemployment or the issue of abortion), to the construction of a "we" as the generalized subject of such diverse demands. The only way to attain such a connection is when they are all directed against a common element seen as the obstacle to attaining a social totality. Such a negative role can be played only by an element of the same social structure (e.g., the actual government or a particular group) against which a new structure attempts to identify itself. Otherness cannot be *originally* external to the attempted totality, because then it would not be involved in the process of identity formation: it would remain, we might say, *indifferent difference*, unrelated to the desire for identity. For otherness to play such a constitutive role, it must be based on something that *belongs* to the domain of demanding identification, but is *excluded* from the task. "The only possibility of having a true outside," says Laclau, "is not simply one more, neutral element but an excluded one, something that the totality expels from itself in order to constitute itself" (2005, p. 70). The first step in the construction of social identity is, thus, the *exclusion* of a given element of the social which becomes the "constitutive outside" for the identity-to-come. Claiming that all identities are set against something, Laclau continues, and at the same time counters Hegel, for whom identity is built in a *logical* relation to difference. This is why it is possible, according to Hegel, to re-absorb difference in a gesture of synthesis which restores totality. In Laclau, social identities do not follow *logical* relations between concepts (or essences), and, therefore, society cannot construe itself by overcoming its contradictions by logical means. Therefore, Hegel's notion of logical difference must be replaced by that of exclusion. The excluded element is part of the heterogeneous social, but it does not take part in the construction of the new identity (which does not mean that it will not be included in the construction of *another* identity). Consequently, identity will never become complete: lack will always be there, society will never be reconciled, it will always be deprived of stable identity, and its precarious totality must be secured politically, by relations of hegemony.

As I have mentioned, unfulfilled demands are diverse, and there is no conceptual framework in which they can be united. For instance, demands for higher pensions, lower income taxes, strict immigration rules, and a ban on pornography may be expressed by the same populist movement. However, once they are addressed against a force (location, institution, etc.) seen as the obstacle on the way to fullness, they gain a universal feature – they are all articulated against the same excluded element, and, thus, they become *equivalent* in relation to one another. The "chain of equivalence" of such demands becomes the first element of the emerging identity. As there is no logical or conceptual framework through which such equivalent articulation can achieve positive identification, the task has to be completed rhetorically. Such a rhetorical operation is possible thanks to the fact that the construction of equivalence, described above, can be identified with the rhetorical figure of *metonymy*, which denotes the possibility of naming an object by a word representing something which is contiguous, or associated with this object. Diverse political demands can, thus, be articulated not because they are "essentially" similar, but because they all share the feature of "being against" the same object.

The next step is possible because of the double status of each demand articulated in such equivalent connections. They are at the same time particular (they represent given demands, like a ban on immigration or lower taxes) and universal (they are all against the same force, and, thus, equivalent one to another). This universal aspect makes it possible for the desire for fullness (which Laclau calls "the populist demand") to be represented. For this purpose, one element of the chain has to be given the role of representing the whole. The ontologically impossible but politically necessary totality may find its representation when one of the particular differences (one of many demands in the chain of equivalence) "assumes the representation of an incommensurable totality" (2005, p. 70). Being invested with the meaning of the whole, a particular demand is, thus, "elevated to the dignity of the Thing," in Freudian terms (Laclau 2005). Becoming a signifier of the desired totality, it transcends its original meaning. As Laclau says, it becomes *an empty signifier*. Its main role is that of naming the impossible totality. In other words, the name of the particular becomes the name of fullness. In rhetorical terms, such a transition from the particular to the universal is a *synecdoche*, and in psychoanalysis it is represented by the notion of *cathexis*. Linking such a function to the repertoire of tropes in classical rhetoric, Laclau identifies it with the figure of *catachresis*, which denotes the use of any adjacent term to name that which has no proper name (further, I will discuss this issue in more detail). Once created and elevated, an empty signifier/catachresis works backward on the whole chain of equivalence so that all its elements become united "in the name" of that signifier. Thus, identity is temporarily established. One example given by Laclau is when the demand for creating free trade unions started to represent all demands (economic, political, related to labor conditions and public housing policies, etc.) in the Polish revolution against the Communist government in 1980, and the name of the union thus created (*Solidarność*) became the signifier uniting the whole political movement (Laclau 2005). In political terms, Laclau, following Gramsci, refers to such a representation of totality by the particular as *hegemony* (Laclau and Mouffe 1985; Laclau 1990; 1996; 2000; 2005; 2014). This Gramscian concept is interpreted by Laclau as structurally identical with the trope of catachresis and with the Lacanian concept of *objet petit a* (an accessible object representing the unattainable object of desire).

There are some elements in this highly condensed recapitulation of Laclau's argument that need closer scrutiny here. As I mention frequently, I see educational theories as discourses implicated in the political construction of societies. On their most general level (which one could call "the deepest," had it not been for the fact that, according to Laclau, it is located on what is usually considered the *textual surface*, in the work of signifiers rather than in signified "essences," and in the rhetorics of theories rather than in the depths of their conceptual foundations), they are part of *the political* – of the very ontology of the social. To interpret educational theories as operating in the ontological layers of society, in the "discursive kitchen" where particular demands are articulated and their hegemonies established, and where the conditions for such articulations and hegemonization are forged, one needs to give more attention to the rhetorical aspects of identity as they are described by Laclau.

Tropes and strategies: Toward educational analyses

Laclau's theory has been discussed, applauded, and criticized for a long time. In spite of criticism, it remains one of the most appreciated political ontologies, and its explanatory potential is praised also by its critics (cf. Critchley 2004; Kaplan 2010; Žižek 2008; Butler and Žižek, in: Butler, Laclau and Žižek 2000). Some critics address issues which I find directly important for the application of this theory in educational studies. Others speak of more technical problems, but some of these inspire answers that go beyond the original shape of the theory and open interesting perspectives for educational analyses as well. The questions I raise here concern issues of normativity, relations between metonymies, metaphors, catachreses, and concepts, and a certain deficit in processual, or strategic, aspects of rhetorics (like the traditional concern with persuasion), which links to the issue of rhetorical agency (Kaplan 2010).

As any complex idea that evolves over time, Laclau's theory contains concepts that gradually change in meaning, and this causes certain difficulties in reconstructing its conceptual apparatus. A good example is one of the main concepts of this theory – the notion of the empty signifier. It appears in Laclau's work in two versions. Sometimes (e.g., 1996) Laclau defines it very simply as a signifier without the signified, a detached term which points to no referent. We might take this minimal understanding as sufficiently functional in explaining why notions such as "democracy" or "a knowledge-based society," when used as brands of political identities and as mobilizing slogans, are empty in the sense of not pointing to clearly defined referents. This is not only because of technical difficulties in defining their meaning, but also for the sake of their pragmatic functionality. Clearly defined, they would lose their mobilizing potential; they would collapse into mere differences in chains of other signifiers. Clear definitions need clear borders, and this would hamper the possibility of articulating diverse issues as belonging to broad political agendas. As society is not determined by any single instance in a positive way (Laclau 1990; 2000; 2005), such representations cannot have a clear conceptual form; they will always elude attempts at definition, or else they would lose their integrating potential. At the same time, however, in more detailed considerations, Laclau points to a "heavier," ontological (and sometimes theological) meaning of the empty signifier (Laclau 1996; 2004; 2005; 2014). The empty signifier signifies that which cannot be represented for *ontological* reasons: a fullness, a totality of society, or divinity. This understanding is supported by references to Lacanian psychoanalysis. For instance, Laclau (2005) maintains that the idea of hegemony in Gramsci is identical, in structural terms, to *objet petit a* in Lacan: in both cases, fullness is impossible, and the desire of such unattainable totality must be invested in something particular. For this reason, it always fails.

Emptiness in signification connects to other questions that need to be mentioned in this context. First is the problem of arbitrariness in the process of representation. Is it really so that *any* demand, and, thus, any signifier can be "elevated to the dignity of the Thing" and serve the need of identification? In pedagogical terms, are we indeed free to construe students' identities "in the name" of *any* demand and around *any* symbol? Their emptiness seems to allow for such arbitrariness, but Laclau (2004; 2005; 2014) gives a negative answer to such a presupposition and makes it clear that existing normative orders constitute limits to the arbitrariness of investments leading to identity. An important discussion on this issue was initiated by Simon Critchley (2002; 2004) who posed the question of a "normative deficit" in Laclau's theory, which prompted Laclau to develop his position on this issue significantly. The question behind this discussion is not only that of the political efficiency of Laclau's conception, which was the main concern for Critchley, but also that of the ability of Laclau's theory to distinguish between ethically acceptable and unacceptable hegemonies (Laclau 2005). In ontological terms, the process of identity construction in fascist movements does not differ much from that taking place, for instance, in liberal ones – all of them need exclusion, equivalence, and the radical investment of the meaning of totality into a particular demand. The question is, therefore, whether Laclau's theory can be used, for instance, by extreme right populists to organize their campaigns more effectively. Laclau's answer is that, however radical in ontological terms, hegemonic investments always operate within historically specific normative orders which constitute limits to their arbitrariness. The threat of "anything goes" in the process of construing social totalities would, thus, be possible only

> if we just started with signifiers of emptiness/fullness and were offered a series of alternative normative orders as possible objects of ethical investment. . . . But the ethical subject constituted through the investment is never an unencumbered moral subject; it fully participates in a normative order not all of which is put into question at the same time. That is the reason why moral argument can . . . appeal to shared values which are presented as grounds for preferring some courses of action rather than other. Not all ethical investments are possible at the given time.
>
> (Laclau 2004, p. 287)

The difference between the ethical and the normative in this discussion echoes that between the ontological and the ontic of which I spoke before. In other words, ethics relates to the absent fullness, to the "positive reverse" of the faults in social structure, while norms dwell in particular ontic conditions. This is why "the ethical subject" is constituted by way of investing such a desire for fullness into particular norms, which are – to paraphrase Laclau – always there, and they are binding for the subject.

The argument provided in the answer to Critchley's question mentioned above is convincing as long as we stay within the domain of politics, especially when we speak of democratic rather than authoritarian or totalitarian societies. The situation is not so clear when the question is transferred to the domain of education. If we take into account the fact that schools do, in some dimensions of their work, *design* their own normative settings, sometimes simply different from, but sometimes clearly directed *against* the normative orders operating in their social milieus (after all, one of the goals assigned to education is to change societies), the question of normative limits to identity, when identity is construed pedagogically, seems to require a more precise consideration; it calls for answers situated somewhere between Laclau's ethics (as they concern the desire of fullness) and normativity (as historically specific rules organizing the social, and in the case of education, occasionally challenged and reformulated). The histories of colonial education, or the cases of Rousseau and the pedagogies of "educating society" discussed in previous chapters, clearly point to the possibility of radical reconstructions of identities, both in their personal and political dimensions, *in spite of* normative orders prevailing in given societies. In other words, *in schools we can do it*: to a certain degree, one can invent normative orders that are capable of embodying the ethical demand of social fullness in ways different from the given. This can be illustrated by the banal example of educational games which promote cooperation rather than competition, while it is the norms of competition which structure capitalist societies. Educational theory cannot, thus, be indifferent to the normative dimension of *arbitrary ethical investments* (i.e., not determined by either the ethical itself, as long as that is "empty," or by the existing normative orders) as allowing for both, to repeat the example, fascist and liberal consequences. The answer provided by Laclau, adequate as it is for historically specific political projects and for hegemonies understood as emerging through the bottom-up development of popular movements, needs elaboration when it is applied to educational settings where, to a certain degree, identities may be created by design. Of course, one could say that such radical reconstructions are also part of the normative order which always allows for alternatives, especially in liberal democracies where political ideas are relatively freely created and circulated. Radical change is then a matter of shifts between the center and the margins of political discourse, rather than of abrupt intrusions of normatively unacceptable projects; nevertheless, such shifts still need normative justification more precise than that provided in Laclau's answer to Critchley's criticism. In another text (Szkudlarek 2007),

I discuss this problem in more detail, pointing to the moment of exclusion as the site of possible normative interrogations that permit the judging of the ethical consequences of given projects of identity *before* they are capable of fulfilling their hegemonic promises. The suggestion is that being attentive to *who is being excluded* from claims to identity may help to envision the shape of the emerging hegemony even before the demands are articulated into a chain of equivalence, and that political and pedagogical interventions into the process of identity construction may be effective at this very initial stage of metonymic articulation. Elsewhere (2013), I point to the question of a "third instance" between the ethical and the normative as bridging their radical distance, which might be helpful in developing some grounds for "judging the emptiness"; in other words, for assessing possible consequences of referring to diverse signifiers of absent fullness in the construction of projected identities. Juxtaposing the works of Ernesto Laclau with those of Chantal Mouffe, I point to the instance of *forms of the social* that can be both identified in given historical contexts and invented as non-existent, desired projects. In the latter case, such instances are close to Laclau's impossible totalities, but they can be presented as conceptually coherent projects that can be compared and ethically evaluated. The example of Mouffe's ethical preference for agonism as a *better form* of antagonism shows that the ethical/normative gap can be narrowed (Szkudlarek 2013).

Apart from allowing for the analyses of education in terms of the construction of identities functional to given political projects (which subscribes to the ontic dimension of politics), Laclau's theory provides for significant insight as to the role of education in the *ontological* dimension of politics ("the political"). In my understanding, such ontological work of education can be seen in the mundane, daily practices of schooling related to meaning-making activities in the classroom: the construction of curricula, teaching methodologies, the topics and methods of classroom debates; in short, the content of teaching and that which Jan Masschelein and Marten Simons (2013a) call "public pedagogic forms," with their specific rhetorics, can be analyzed as productive of resources of the rhetorical construction of society. Elsewhere (2007) I suggest that schools can be seen in this context as "factories of empty signifiers." This suggestion needs empirical research to be verified. Before such research is possible, though, it needs some theoretical elaboration. This, in turn, connects to the need for discussing the possibility of empty signifiers being purposefully, or systematically, *produced*.

In the previously mentioned "heavier" understanding of empty signifiers, like in the analysis of populism, Laclau sees them as catachreses pointing to the impossible fullness of society created *ad hoc* in the course of populist mobilization, when particular demands (and words that denote them) are invested with the meaning of such fullness. In other words, in populist movements, empty signifiers are not "fabricated"; they emerge gradually as the effect of the articulation of diverse demands which need singular representation. However, Laclau does not deny the idea of such signifiers being *produced*, and he speaks of such production in many places: for instance, one of the chapters in *On Populist Reason* is titled "The 'People' and the Discursive Production of Emptiness," and in another text (2004) he points to "*a series of terms* whose semantic consists in pointing to an absent fullness, to an absolutely empty space deprived of formal determination" (2004, p. 286, italics added). He mentions such terms as "justice," "truth," "faithfulness," "honesty," "goodness," etc. Explaining the relation of such terms to social experience, Laclau says that they are negations ("positive reverse," 2004, p. 287) of the experience of lack, of the absence of justice, truth, etc. as a constant feature of the social. However, one should note that such terms do exist *before* we experience injustice or dishonesty, and that their emptiness must have been produced independently of, and prior to, such particular experiences. In other words, if we have "a series of terms" which denote impossible fullness, it is not only so that what is activated in the process of populist mobilization are particular demands, rooted in historically specific experience of deprivation, but also *these terms* – as historical and cultural constructs – as such. The apparently trivial question I want to address here is how people engaged in such political activity *know* that such terms represent the desired and impossible fullness. I believe that it is here that Laclau's political theory definitely needs *pedagogical supplementation*, and that without such supplement its ontological potential is incomplete. To some degree, this belief is similar to Michael Kaplan's (2010) observation that Laclau's focus on structural aspects of discourse (and, thus, a narrow understanding of rhetoric, reduced to tropology) makes his theory incomplete in terms of analyzing rhetorical strategies, including those of *choosing* a particular signifier of the missing fullness as the name of the desired identity. In the context of normative orders being not only respected, but also projected, in education, these are indeed fundamental questions. This problem relates to the issue of rhetorical agency (i.e., to the means that can be used by political agents to construe hegemonies and to construe objects of exclusion, the "enemies" of the people, as the condition of defining the borders of totality). Laclau's theory, understood by Kaplan as strongly informed by structuralist methodology and an understanding of rhetoric reduced to tropology, neglecting, for instance, the issue of pragmatics, the role of discursive forms, and the contemporary deconstructions of the classic distinctions between metonymies, metaphors, catachreses, and concepts (Kaplan refers here to Jacques Derrida and Paul de Man), seems to give no solid ground for such agency. Even though Laclau points to the "shading" of "'contiguity' into 'analogy,' 'metonymy' into 'metaphor,'" and calls hegemony "the movement from metonymy to metaphor, from *contingent* articulation to *essential* belonging" (Laclau 2014, p. 63), according to Kaplan, "his theory of politics *requires* metaphor, metonymy and catachresis to retain a degree of the specificity they derive from their inscription within the classical rhetorical tradition" (Kaplan 2010, p. 270). This somewhat rigid structure is claimed to leave no room for rhetorical agency or for discussing rhetorical efficiency. In a way, not surprisingly so, if one takes into account its strongly structural character and the fact that in social sciences "structure" has always been discussed as making "agency" problematic. As Kaplan notes, Laclau describes the processes of identification as spontaneous (to remind, his analyses are based on the histories of populist movements), using passive voice, which stresses the lack of rhetorical agency, or rational strategy behind such processes.[2] In short, as Kaplan says, Laclau's impressive theory needs to be supplemented with a more careful examination of rhetorical efficiency and of diverse discursive forms. An important factor missed by Laclau is, according to Kaplan, the instance of *iterability* as stabilizing the arbitrary relation between the sign and the object. In other words, according to Kaplan, identity, which appears to be the sole effect of *naming* in Laclau's theory (let us add, also in Žižek's, before his divorce with Laclau's thought [Žižek 1989]), is, in fact, stabilized by endless iterations, by repetitions of such couplings.

Even though I strongly admire the criticized structural character of Laclau's theory, I want to use Kaplan's call for supplementing it with a more dynamic understanding of rhetoric to suggest that the issues of discursive forms and iterations clearly point to *the constitutive role of education in the construction of the political*, and in the pedagogical production of empty signifiers in particular. What I am aiming at is seeing the school as a place where certain terms are being turned into "empty signifier prefabs" by means of *specifically pedagogic forms of discourse*. Once produced as such, they supply the repository of terms applicable in the construction of identity. To describe educational rhetoric as working in this ontological field, following Kaplan, one needs to supplement Laclau's structural model with a more processual account on the operation of metonymies, metaphors, and catachreses as – and this aspect is important in the light of my prior observation concerning the dependence of identification on historically construed "terms that point to absent fullness" – operating in the domain of culture. In other words, I aim at seeing schools as places of "a strategic use of language," of methodical construction, iteration, circulation and stabilization, as well as deconstructions of representations, where some of them are turned into "empty signifier prefabs." I believe that pedagogical rhetorics are indispensable for the operation of hegemonic identification, and their understanding is crucial for the theory of the political. To provide for concepts that allow for such a description, I will try to supplement Laclau's model of identity with Umberto Eco's analysis of transitions between metonymies, metaphors, and catachreses, and of their relation to what he calls "cultural codes" (Eco 1984).

Before I turn to Eco, however, I want to note that we have a long tradition of discussing such constructions in educational theories, but they have been articulated in another language which – in order to give more substance to the idea of schools fabricating empty signifiers – needs to be translated into Laclau's categories. Searching for analogies to Laclau's notion of "terms whose semantic consists in pointing to an absent fullness" (2004, p. 286) one should turn to the role ascribed to *values* in education (Szkudlarek 2008). One such analogy is apparent: values are never fully attainable, which means that they never cease to be striven for; they are always demanded; they *oblige* as ideal standards of human behavior, but they never "fully exist" or are fully incarnated in particular objects. The idealistic tradition holds that they dwell in a separate world of ideas. Truth, love, and justice are ideals rather than objects of our daily experience, and the mode of their existence in material realities is being recognized in, or assigned to, particular events or situations, which clearly corresponds to the notion of investment, or cathexis, in Laclau. Something or somebody "embodies," "represents," or is "a paragon of" truth or justice. Second, in educational practice, we may draw the students toward the awareness of the existence of values only *through the particular:* through the exposition and analysis of specific objects (of art, for instance), events, and their conflictual structure (as in tragedy), behaviors, or biographies. Third, apart from being impossible to be accomplished and being accessible only via the particular, values have one more fundamental feature: they are *important,* or "worth" being striven for. In Laclau's language, they can be represented as demands. My point here is that all we do under the label of value education can be analyzed not only as pertinent to the formation of individuals, which we traditionally do in educational theories, but also as related to the *production of terms which are applicable as empty signifiers in the construction of political identities.*

At the first glance, an obvious difference between Laclau's empty signifiers and values in the discourse of education is, so to say, the vector of their operation. While it is directed upwards in Laclau ("elevation" of particular demands "to the dignity of the Thing"), it descends from the ideal to the mundane (incarnation, embodiment) in the idealist axiological and pedagogical tradition. However, when Laclau speaks of the ethical, he refers to similarly descending metaphors.

> [T]he primary ethical experience is the experience of a lack: it is constituted by the distance between what is and what ought to be. I have also asserted – and that is what approaches the ethical experience to the mystical one – that the object bridging that distance does not have a content of its own because it is a positive reverse of something lived as negative. Now we can advance one more step in the argument and assert that any positive moral evaluation consists in *attributing to a particular content the role of a bearer of one of the names of fullness.* ... Here we have *investment* in an almost literal financial sense: the relevance of the term is greatly increased by making it the embodiment of a fullness totally transcending it.
>
> (Laclau 2004, p. 287, italics added)

The relation between the particular and the universal (i.e., representing the impossible fullness) is, thus, bi-directional, which means that we have to imagine a reservoir, a cultural repository of empty signifiers (of terms capable of representing absent fullness) that can be "taken down" as terms representing impossible totalities and can work as "elevators" lifting the particular up to "the dignity of the Thing." These are, to a large extent, the same terms that operate in the process of pedagogical construction of individual identities. To illustrate this connection, one may refer to the tradition of *Geisteswissenschaftliche Pädagogik* (later also known as *Kulturpädagogik* – *humanistic* or *cultural* pedagogy, respectively) developed in Germany and spread throughout Continental Europe at the beginning of the twentieth century. Its main representatives (Eduard Spranger, Theodor Litt, Herman Nohl and Wilhelm Fittner in Germany, or Sergiusz Hessen, Bogdan Suchodolski, and Bohdan Nawroczyński in Poland), inspired by the nineteenth-century debate on the status of the humanities, especially by the works of Friedrich Schleiermacher and Wilhelm Dilthey and by philosophical works concerning the understanding of the Spirit (*der Geist* – the term that nowadays can be represented by *culture*), with Hegel and Humboldt as the most important authorities, developed a theory of education (*Bildung*) understood as the formation of the spiritual structure of the individual through the acquisition of values (Milerski 2003). Spranger created a typology of personality built on a typology of values related to different forms of cultural activities. In other words, to the *content* of culture, or, in the language of that tradition, to particular objectifications of the Spirit. The typology included theoretical, economic, aesthetic, religious, political, and social personalities linked to the values of truth, utility ("the useful"), beauty ("form and harmony"), sanctity ("unity"), power, and love of people (Spranger 1928). This led to the curricular strategy of exposing the variety of *Lebensformen* (ways of life) to the learners so that they have a chance to exclude, from their further studies and visions of their personal future, those ways that do not "resonate" with their personal preferences, and to integrate these preferences in terms of a "chosen" value. Translating these assumptions into the language of Laclau's theory, one may say that liberal education (*Bildung*), aimed at helping students to integrate their particular individual experiences into the "structure of the self" organized around a given value, follows the stages of exclusion ("I do not feel like being an artist or a scientist"), equivalence ("everything I like and feel good at is kind of more practical, it's nothing like 'science'"), investment/cathexis ("the project on the school budget was really something, I felt I can be better than other guys in planning"), and retroactive integration/identification through naming ("I will be an economist"). By no means is this trivial example meant to reduce the structure of Laclau's theory to the banality of progress in personal identification. Taking into account the fact that Laclau borrows some of his concepts from psychoanalysis, possible homologies between the processes of creating political and personal identities should not be surprising at all, and it is not my aim to enumerate such similarities. My intention is different: I merely want to point to the rich experience that schools have in working with diverse tactics of identification, as well as in working with "terms that point to absent fullness." Moreover, I assume that such tactics have not been adequately described in all their aspects, and, first of all, not in a way that could make such descriptions applicable in the analyses of political ontology. What seems unique to this experience, and what can really shed light on one of the controversies discussed in Laclau's theory, is the fact that pedagogical construction of identity indeed involves a moment denied to the political one by Laclau: a moment in which one proceeds *from the ethical* (the desire of identity) to its precarious and particular fulfillment (the student's "discovery" of being an economist) through the very important stage of *choosing a normative order* (a particular course or discipline of studies), or of *inventing* one (particular curricular experiences that can be designed for the student, or for a cohort of students, to achieve specific goals and to "become somebody"). As I said before in my comment on Laclau's statement that one cannot invest the ethical demand into chosen normative orders, *in schools we can do it*. This possibility only strengthens the importance of the normative in theorizing the construction of identity, both in education and in politics.[3]

There is also one more important aspect of schools' working with values. How do they manage to associate values (as abstract ideas) with particular terms? How do they create axiological signifiers? This seems an ultimately important question to our understanding of the construction of social ontologies. To recall Laclau's phrase, "a series of terms that point to absent fullness" is a cultural phenomenon; they are specific terms, words indeed, that need to be *construed* as pointing to "absent fullness" rather than to somebody's particular experience. How do we create such *terms of values* – how do we make particular signifiers *empty* and *important* at the same time?

To large an extent, this is an empirical question. One needs to analyze textbooks, to record classroom discussions, to analyze arguments and explanations raised in the discussions on literature or cinema, to photograph and analyze school exhibitions, and to read justifications for best student awards. In short, to research school discourse, both in its structural and processual dimensions, in all aspects that involve the work of terms pertaining to values. I assume that initially they may appear in the horizon of a child's experience as words of purely behavioral significance, occasionally used by adult others to steer one's personal behavior, with meanings provisionally guessed and postponed to be tested for clarity on other occasions; that they are recalled in classes, which may be hoped to elucidate doubts as to their meaning, but that hope is failed again because in discussions other students bring experiences completely different from one's own, while they still label them with the same term; that extensive readings in later stages of education increase the complexity and reduce whatever clarity such terms have, gradually positioning them in an empty place surrounded by floating arrays of meanings. And so on. Terms of values have long histories of attempts at clarification countered by pedagogically controlled deconstructions, of simultaneous pressure on being discussed and on such discussions not being conclusive; of vagueness, curiosity, disappointment, and deference. While we use them in classroom practice, such terms are gradually abstracted (detached from concrete referents) and made more complex at the same time. They gradually attain representation which is at the same time negative ("true friendship *is not* about going out together . . . listening to your secrets . . . sharing your music . . . helping each other. . .") and transcending that which can be named (". . . it can be all that, but it is *something more*"). The endless discussions and endlessly repeated "pedagogically productive" topics for student essays (Is public good superior to personal happiness? What is responsibility? Has the restoration of the sciences and arts contributed to the purification of morals?[4]) multiply answers and raise new questions, leaving the students with no conclusions and with the feeling that the question is unanswerable; however, the issue is ultimately important and needs more investigation. Terms of values are, thus, *emptied* of particular, experiential meanings (they no longer mean what anybody initially thought they did) and remain impossible to be defined. The endless practice of repetition, multiplication, and decontextualization, with the inevitable boredom and fatigue that makes one stop demanding more precise definitions, keeps such signifiers empty. Simultaneously, the occasions when such terms are used often become ritualized. The timbre of a teacher's voice is changed, the posture is different, the eyes are looking up – we are speaking of patriotism; or of the eternal beauty of Mona Lisa. Terms pointing to absent fullness get canonized; they become sacred and unquestionably elevated. Initially, they are "empty" in a very technical sense: through multiplicity of experiential referents, then through repetitiveness, boredom, or the impossibility of demanding their clear meaning, they become mere words of importance. Then they start representing that very *impossibility* of final definitions, of agreement, of commonplace understanding – they point to the very transcendence of meaning, to the fact that there is a "beyond" which transmits the true and unspeakable sense of that which "really" matters.

Indeed, there is a *series* (not a system!) of such terms, and I assume that they are produced in schools, in churches, in public media – in the institutions where their particular meanings are articulated and at the same time transcended towards abstract, decontextualized, ready-to-use signifiers of *whatever* identity. It is as if "words of importance" were floating above our heads in the cultural repository, in a shared *cloud*, ready to be pulled down to signify our longing for better selves and better worlds-to-come.

There is another theoretical issue that connects to this vision of pedagogically produced and publicly shared clouds of signifiers applicable in hegemonic practices. This issue may, indirectly, relate to the previously mentioned question regarding the alleged normative deficit of Laclau's theory. If I may remind, one of the aspects of this deficit stems from the ontological dimension of radical investments. In other words, Laclau's model does not allow for distinguishing between "good" vs. "bad" identifications on the ontological level. As long as all investments are radical, which, in fact, means arbitrary and unconditioned, such distinctions can be made only on a historically specific *normative* (not ethical/ontological) level. In other words, the theoretical model of hegemony allows for analyzing *any* hegemony and provides no conceptual instruments for preventing it from being used as a tool for, say, a fascist revolution; Laclau delegates those who search for such instruments to the normative as it currently is. As I suggested before, one might implant such additional tools into Laclau's model, especially when it is applied in educational theory. They may operate in the first stages of the construction of hegemony, when a "constitutive outside" is created by means of excluding certain demands from the process of identification. This is when one should be attentive to *whom* and *what* is being excluded on the way to identity. Such negative criteria can be helpful in envisioning the shape of the emerging totality (Szkudlarek 2007). This issue leads to more questions concerning the very construction of the model, which will require a discussion on the nature of tropes that organize its dynamic.

My initial intention behind such interpretation of rhetorical figures productive of Laclau's ontology was testing whether it is indeed impossible to connect it – for reasons I will explain in a while – to some elements of the Hegelian dialectic of identity As I have mentioned, Laclau is very decisive in pitting his theory against Hegel and Marx, which is justified, among other reasons, by exclusions of the heterogeneous *made* by these two thinkers in their conceptual models (peoples without history in Hegel and *Lumpenproletariat* in Marx are left outside their dialectics), which makes it impossible to properly *theorize* exclusion as a condition of hegemony. Laclau's position in this respect has been challenged by Žižek. Apart from following Marx in claiming place for economic determination (as "determination of the last instance" [Žižek 2008]) in the theory of hegemony, which would help to explain current political struggles where it is not so much the issue of identity as it is the one, again, of overt economic exploitation that mobilizes political movements on a global scale, Žižek (1994) has also provided for a strong theoretical argument which suggests the possibility of bridging the theory of hegemony with the Hegelian dialectic. In brief, Žižek shows how hegemony, including the retroactive gesture of naming, which "grounds the foundation" for a new identity and, thus, articulates the so-far disconnected elements into one structure, is present in Hegel's logic of essence. If a common reading of Laclau's theory and of Hegelian dialectic were indeed possible, interesting questions could be asked regarding the ontology of the "cloud," or of the reservoir of empty signifiers. Such questions are important in light of the already addressed issue of normativity. Hegelian dialectic is very precise as regards the relations between concepts in which their "inner" negativity (or incompleteness) is productive of their negations, which are eventually subsumed into the concept so that both positive and negative elements create new entities (syntheses). If one could translate the Hegelian logic of negation into the language of Laclau's rhetoric, it would help to analyze relations *between* the terms of identity, that is to say *within* the cloud of empty signifiers. This will, of course, raise the question of their emptiness: Is it complete? Or "how empty" is it? What interests me in this issue is the question of whether identities achieved through hegemony organized around empty signifiers relate – on the level of such signifiers – to *other* possible identities. Hardly ever, in democratic societies, do we have a situation of one single claim to totality. Instead, we usually witness competing claims, competing signifiers of competing, alternative totalities. To give an example, in the current (2015–2016) political campaign of the right-wing government of Poland, *public* institutions are re-labeled as *national* institutions, and "nation" replaces "society" in the language of government officials. Both signifiers refer to impossible totality, but is that one and the same totality – or two different ones? Both signifiers are apparently empty, but are they completely so? Indeed, the connection between the signifier ("the nation") and the chain of particular demands and relevant policies (provisions for Polish families aimed at stimulating birth rates, taxing international capital, attempts at controlling the media and cultural production institutions to stimulate patriotic attitudes, etc.) are established, as Kaplan observes, by iterations: this is the most striking feature of the new public language. The constantly repeated phrases of "Polish families," "the nation," and "good change" in collocations with controversial elements of parliamentary bills quickly redefine the structure of public discourse. But is it not so that the very terminological shift from "the society" to "the nation" foretells such change? If we take these terms as concepts, the one of "society" does not necessarily position itself against "other societies," while the one of "the nation" quickly lands in the field occupied by *other* nations. Returning to the theoretical level, are "nations" and "societies" *only* empty signifiers speaking to impossible totalities, or are some of such terms, at the same time, concepts that carry with them their specific denotations and collocations? In other words, the question is whether the success of a populist movement, crystallized in the form of hegemony organized by a given symbol, is capable – on that symbolic level – of *provoking* its own negation. Does its signifier anyhow relate to other signifiers "waiting for their turn" in being used for political struggles? Can it be *negated* by another signifier? These questions aim at testing the possibility of using the same theoretical model for analyzing hegemony based on heterogeneous demands and analyzing *ideological struggles* between signifiers representing competing claims to totality.

It is clear that clouds of empty signifiers cannot be analyzed in terms of Hegelian dialectic as such, without challenging the "emptiness" of signifiers and without testing Hegel's theory for such possible application, for instance, following Žižek's interpretations. However, as I have mentioned before, the status of empty signifiers is, according to Laclau, that of catachreses. I want to follow this issue now. If the instance of repositories of empty signifiers can indeed be introduced into the theory of hegemony, and if one wants to better define their role in the construction of identity, one should give more attention to the features of catachresis and to the relation between catachresis, other tropes, and concepts.

The notion of catachresis appears in Laclau's texts relatively late. In older texts, he tends to speak of *metaphor* as the trope connecting heterogeneous elements in identity, while in more recent ones he usually speaks, in a similar context, of catachresis. At the same time, the issue of metaphor is kept alive in his recent publications (2014) as well. In *New Reflections on the Revolution of our Time* (1990) we read of *mythical subjects* (where myths add the absent, totalizing element to social reality) which are at the same time "constitutively metaphorical subjects" (1990, p. 62), which means that they have to live in "failed" structures where diverse meanings have to be metaphorically articulated. It is also in this context, inherent to Laclau's writings, that the relation between catachresis and metaphor needs to be addressed.

Patricia Parker (1990) provides an overview of how the relation between metaphor and catachresis was understood in the history of rhetoric. She starts with Quintilian's definition of catachresis as "the practise of adapting the nearest available term to describe something for which no actual [i.e., proper] term exists" (Parker 1990, p. 60). This way of defining catachresis is close to Laclau's, who refers (quoting Parker) to Cicero's description of language as "too poor" in its variety of terms to cover all things in the world. This shortage of words means that proper terms are "abused" so that they can denote that which has no name. As Laclau says, this idea should be given a stronger meaning: it is not merely the insufficiency of words, but the ontological *impossibility and necessity* of naming things which are "essentially unnameable" that is constitutive of language (Laclau 2005, p. 71). "In classical rhetoric," says Laclau, "a figural term which cannot be substituted by a literal one, was called a catachresis. . . . If the empty signifier arises from the need to name an object which is both impossible and necessary, . . . the hegemonic operation will be catachrestical through and through" (2005, pp. 71–72). However, in Quintilian and Cicero themselves, as Parker notes, there is no consistency as to how the relation between catachresis and metaphor is understood. While the difference between these tropes seems initially clear and grounds in the issue of the absence vs. the presence of a proper term, whence the idea of "necessary" catachreses and "decorative" metaphors, the fact that catachresis is defined as "abusing" the terms opens the way for extending its range to cases when a *metaphor* is "abusive" (e.g., too far-fetched, banal, or dead). Returning to Parker's typology, there are approaches which assert that languages evolved from "necessity" to "adornment," which turns catachresis into an archaic and nowadays "abusive" trope, and there are ones which extend the notion of catachresis to the whole domain of signification. Also, both metaphor and catachresis are seen as two specific modes of transference, and there is a Derridean idea of catachresis being an undecidable which – by its very presence in the repertoire of linguistic devices – threatens the distinction between literal and figurative uses of language (Parker 1990). Even though Laclau uses the term as close to its original meaning as possible (i.e., as a figure representing that which has no proper name and thus *cannot* be represented), he moves toward a somewhat totalizing understanding of catachresis where it becomes synonymous with rhetoricity as such (Laclau 2005).

One of the ways this trope was understood in its long history was that of a "dead metaphor," of a metaphor being crystallized into a quasi-concept in which its very metaphoricity is erased and forgotten because of its coupling with a specific referent. Structurally, "a leg of the table" is a metaphor (it connects elements belonging to diverse semantic fields), but pointing, as a sole signifier, to a specific object, it operates like a concept. In this sense, catachresis cannot be seen only as linked to metaphor, but also as a bridge between metaphors and concepts.

In his considerations on the semantics of metaphor, Umberto Eco (1984) connects metonymy, metaphor, and catachresis (here understood in a more narrow sense than in Laclau) in a structure where they form a sequence of transitions within the semantic system. Eco argues that metaphor is grounded in metonymies, and that the possibility of metaphorization and of linguistic creativity in general – including the possibility of changing the codes of culture – resides in the nature of the language. What connects its elements and makes linguistic creativity possible are cultural conventions which provide the language with networks of "arbitrarily stipulated contiguities" (Eco 1984, p. 78).

> The problem of the creativity of language emerges . . . each time that language – in order to designate something that culture has not yet assimilated . . . – must invent combinatory possibilities or semantic couplings not anticipated by the code. Metaphor, in this sense, appears as a new semantic coupling not preceded by any stipulation of the code (but which generates a new stipulation of the code).
>
> (Eco 1984, p. 69)

In this theory, catachresis is something like a late (or dead) metaphor, a metaphor that lost its creative novelty and started to work as part of the cultural code, as a culturally established collocation. "The metaphor, once it has become usual, enters as part of the code and in the long run can fix itself in a *catechresis*. . . . The fact remains, however, that the substitution took place because of the existence, in the code, of connections and therefore contiguities. This would lead us to state that the metaphor rests on a metonymy" (p. 79).

The sequence of metonymy, metaphor, and catachresis seems to reflect the same order, and their relations are based on very similar structural rules as those described by Laclau in the move from equivalence to identity. What Eco brings into this structure is a slightly different description of the internal logic of this process. According to Eco, metaphor (and hence, also catachresis) is formed as a *leap* in the chain of metonymies, by the "short circuit of a pre-established path" (p. 78). That path is formed by metonymic contiguities that, in Eco, can occur on the levels of signifiers and of signifieds. On the level of metonymies, connections can be built not only on semantic grounds, but also on factual judgments related to extra-linguistic experiences. In Laclau, there seems to be no ground for such materiality of contiguities: articulation of demands occurs only on a negative basis, in relation to the excluded element of the social. With all necessary restrictions and reservations, however, we may generally say that Eco and Laclau share a similar view of how change comes to society: through the invention of new couplings that link heterogeneous elements related through metonymic contiguity. Where, as I think, we have some added value in relation to Laclau's theory is, first, in Eco's observation that metaphor is formed as a leap in the chain in metonymies; in other words, that it starts in a horizontal move within the chain of equivalence. Second, that these elements that may eventually be coupled in metaphor (and in catachresis in Laclau) need to share something in the connotations of cultural code (or something *material* if one includes the level of signifieds into the model). Third, there is some semiotic economy of metaphorization, and fourth – the interesting idea of how affect is involved in the process. More must be said about the two latter issues.

Metaphors in Eco can be "good" or "bad." A good, or productive, metaphor can always be explained by filling the gap between its elements with mediating metonymical contiguities. Reading a metaphor, says Eco, demands tracing the chain of metonymies: the metaphor is adequate when we can re-work the chain, when it translates itself to metonymical contiguities (let's say, like when explaining a joke to a slow thinker). This means that there is some internal economy to the process: that is, that the distance between the elements that form a metaphor, measurable by the number of skipped metonymic connections, cannot be too small, because then the metaphor is "obvious" and it does not work as an inspiring element in the semantic system; conversely, such a leap cannot be too large, because then the effect is illegible and the connection cannot be recognized as metaphor at all. As Eco says, creative, or productive metaphor works through *excitation*: its novelty and its productive force, revealing connections previously not perceived, result in fascination and something we could call – after Laclau and Freud – infatuation, a desire to be involved in the sphere of "radiation" of such new articulation. Laclau is very clear in asserting Freud's intuition that the social is based on a kind of love, on libidinal energy that unites individuals (Laclau 2005). Supplementing his theory with Eco's analysis can help to explain how the internal dynamic of transitions from metonymies to metaphors creates such emotional force.

One may thus describe Laclau's ontology as structurally similar to Eco's semantic system. Equivalence of demands is metonymical; it is based on contiguity. We may envision it as a horizontal plateau where particular elements are linkable: as Laclau says, by virtue of their shared opposition toward the excluded; as Eco says, as a consequence of sharing a cultural code. An interesting thing is whether Eco's notion of cultural code may be helpful in predicting the possibility of the articulation of demands. In other words and in Laclau's terms: can *any* demand opposing the excluded join the chain and be accepted as equivalent? Or is it so that some of them are rejected (and perhaps linked to those excluded before) because *no metonymic connections* are possible within a given cultural code? Can anybody who shouts "down with the regime" be included in the new identity – regardless of *why* they shout and what the others think of their reasons? It seems that there are some restrictions to equivalence, perhaps based on what Eco mentions as factual judgments, perhaps pertaining to *ideologies* as specific, cultural codes of articulation. It seems that equivalent demands, to *be* equivalent, must belong to some semantic set defined by rules, or codes of contiguity. What Laclau analyzes can be described as a bottom-up construction of such rules by means of delegating the identity of the whole chain to one of its elements; what we read in Eco can, in turn, be seen as a situation in which such elements are grouped within a "thinkable" unit before the hegemonic process begins.

If this interpretation is correct, and if there is a possibility of using elements of both these theories to analyze the construction of social identities, one could say that the catachretic signifier that represents the universal dimension of demands arrives late, and it is preceded by a *creative metaphor* articulating the metonymically linkable elements of the field in an excitingly original way (see the analysis of the logo of *Solidarność* in Szkudlarek 2011). Such excitation provides the energy necessary for further steps of change, which never occurs without struggle. Only once the connection is established and once it becomes institutionalized as the *name* of a new body does it become catachresis and start working *as if* it were a concept, or a proper name. Its metaphoricity and its contingent origins are thus erased. "When finally, metaphors are transformed into knowledge, they will at last have completed their cycle: they become catachreses. The field has been restructured, semiosis rearranged, and metaphor (from invention which it was) turned into culture" (Eco 1984, p. 87).

What Eco says of excitation as the modus operandi of metaphor can introduce an affective, energetic dimension to the very semiosis of identity formation. Even though for Eco the ground for theoretical analysis lies in literary practices (excitation may then be experienced by writers and their seduced readers), we may also think of it as a creative (or/and destructive) thrill of personal and political change which involves discovering unseen connections, an illumination that reveals possibilities of seeing and thinking differently and of being somebody different. It foretells the joy of re-articulation, self-actualization, of moving from the potential (the contiguous but mentally disconnected, unnamed, unconscious) to the actual: verbalized, given a name, mythically unified as "me" or as "us." Kazimierz Obuchowski, in his psychological research, long ago confirmed the hypothesis that moving "upwards" in cognitive structures (from the concrete and horizontal code of experience toward the vertical and hierarchical code of concepts) results in positive emotions, and that the relation is bi-directional: positive and negative emotions play the steering role in switching between these codes; in terms of the theories discussed here – between seeing the world through metonymic contiguities and through metaphors and catachreses (Obuchowski 1970). Coming back to Laclau's analysis of political identities, we can see why hegemony not only forces people to subordinate, but also *attracts* them, and this process can find its basic explication – parallel to that of libidinal love Laclau continues after Freud, and to the Gramscian contractual explanation – in the very nature of rhetorical devices applied in the process of identity construction. In many places, Laclau acknowledges this rhetorical aspect of affect, but Eco's idea of excitation by creative novelty achieved through the short circuit of signification in metaphor seems to give it a more tangible sense. Then, as we may infer, both subjective and political identification follow the gradual transformation of metaphor into catachresis. Excitation typical of the early stages of identity formation disappears, and the coupling between the new signifier and that which it started to represent (the as yet non-existent identity) crystallizes in a quasi-conceptual representation. To sum up, Eco's theory of metaphor, once translated into the language of Laclau's theory of hegemony, seems to offer a supplementary explication of certain aspects of the process of identification which can possibly expand the explanatory power of this theory of hegemony. Thus expanded, it acquires more tools to explicate educational rhetorics, where the acquisition of cultural codes, and the operations between metonymic contiguities, metaphorical creativity, and the crystallization of concepts organize a vast proportion of what happens in daily discursive exchanges. Analyzing these operations within the structure of Laclau's theory can help to link them to the fundamental issue of the construction of identity in a way which bridges the construction of individuality, culture, and the political and allows for describing their interconnections in one language.

To sum up, I have tried to argue that the concern with normativity in the theory of hegemony, as well the critique of its – as Kaplan puts it – overly structuralist methodology, can inspire answers which, while still operating within the model of Laclau's ontological rhetoric, introduce interesting dynamics into its structure. These intrusions seem complementary, and, in my opinion, there is a chance of integrating them into the theory. The results are promising. On the one hand, in Eco's theory one can find explanatory tools capable of including metonymical contiguities in the domain of the signifieds, if that is needed in particular analyses. The notion of metonymic contiguities being structured by cultural codes may be helpful in more precise analyses of the construction of chains of equivalence, and of cases of particular demands or desires being excluded from such chains. On the other hand, the transitive conception of relations between metonymies, metaphors, catachreses, and concepts – with the latter seen as crystallized, "dead" metaphors/catachreses – creates a space for investigating the relations between empty signifiers, or "terms of values," so that some critique of ideology can be included. Such a possibility is grounded in the fact that catachreses, unlike "living" metaphors, *can* relate to concepts, can be subsumed into hierarchical structures, or, as elements of more abstract representations, enter the sphere of dialectical negations. Both these intrusions seem worth developing, as they seem to have the potential to alleviate the problem with normativity in the theory of hegemony. The attempt at seeing empty signifiers not only in the light of spontaneous articulations and cathectic investment, but also as somewhat stabilized terms stored in repositories of culture, in turn, connects educational rhetorics, with their specific discursive forms, to ontological rhetorics directly involved in the construction of social objectivity.

Notes

1   The reconstruction of Laclau's theory includes fragments of my previous publications: Szkudlarek 2007; 2011; 2013.
2   In another text (Szkudlarek 2011), I discuss the connection between "rhetorical agency" and "efficiency" behind the success of the rhetoric of *Solidarność*, pointing to the artful

construction of the logo of "*Solidarność* by the artist, Jerzy Janiszewski, who, himself, described the meaning of the logo in a way fully congruent with the structure of Laclau's theory, although he was clearly unaware of its existence. This case is not meant to support Kaplan's critique challenging the structure of Laclau's theory in general; rather, it shows that, behind that which appears to be spontaneous identification, there may be somebody's deliberate intention and professional work and that certain semiotic or aesthetic *forms* may indeed be productive of the effect of hegemony. I also claim that empty signifiers are not "entirely empty" and that the way they are construed may be decisive of their rhetorical potential. In fact, Janiszewski's work finds no representation in Laclau's reconstruction of the movement – not only due to the fact that the interview wth Janiszewski was not accessible to Laclau, but also because such individual gestures are, indeed, beyond the range of Laclau's theoretical concepts.

3   In spite of the above reconstruction of a certain homology between the course of iden-
tification in value education and in the construction of political totality, a more careful analysis is needed as regards the similarities and differences between the strategies of pedagogical and political constructions of identity. In education, the process of identification is, in a way, simultaneously composed of the factors of experience and "emer-
gence" on the side of the child, on the one hand, and of control and "expectations," on the other, adult or "systemic" side. As a result, the passage through the process of identification in its educational variety may lead to the *retrospective* "revelation" of the very presence of control and adult expectations that structured the course of formative experience and made the student that which she became as in the exclamation of Rousseau's Emile, quoted in Chapter 2: *What decision have I come to? I have decided to be what you made me* (Rousseau 1921, p. 390). As long as such an announcement can be under-
stood as representing a fairly universal aspect of identity formation, coherent with the Hegelian notion of "grounding the foundation" (Hegel 1873; Žižek 1994) and then its Lacanian modification (Žižek 1989), it remains interesting whether it has an equivalent in the political experience. Can *historical awareness* be understood this way? I am grateful to F. Tony Carusi for raising this question.

4   This was the title of essay competition announced by Academy of Dijon in France in 1749. The competition was won by Jean-Jacques Rousseau, which launched his popu-
larity as a philosopher. See Rousseau (1923).

References

BUTLER, J., LACLAU, E. and ŽIŽEK, S. (2000). *Contingency, Hegemony, Universality: Contemporary Dialogues on the Left*. London: Verso.

CRITCHLEY, S. (2002). Ethics, Politics, and Radical Democracy – A History of Disagreement. *Culture Machine*, 4 [Online]. Available from http://www.culturemachine.net/index.
php/cm/article/view/267/252. [Accessed: 10th December 2015].

CRITCHLEY, S. (2004). Is There a Normative Deficit in the Theory of Hegemony? In CRITCHLEY, S. and MARCHART, O. (eds.) *Laclau. A Critical Reader*. London and New York: Routledge.

ECO, U. (1984). *The Role of the Reader. Explorations in the Semiotics of Texts*. Bloomington: Indiana University Press.

HEGEL, G.F.W. (1873). *The Encyclopaedia of the Philosophical Sciences*. [Online] Available from: https://www.marxists.org/reference/archive/hegel/works/sl/introduction.pdf. [Accessed: 10th December 2015].

INSTON, K. (2010). *Rousseau and Radical Democracy*. London and New York: Continuum.

KAPLAN, M. (2010). The Rhetoric of Hegemony: Laclau, Radical Democracy, and the Rule of Tropes. *Philosophy and Rhetoric*, 43 (3), pp. 253–283.

LACLAU, E. (1990). *New Reflections on the Revolution of our Time*. London:Verso.
LACLAU, E. (1996). *Emancipation(s)*. London:Verso.
LACLAU, E. (2000). Identity and Hegemony: The Role of Universality in the Construction of Political Logic. In BUTLER, J., LACLAU, E. and ŽIŽEK, S. (eds.) *Contingency, Hegemony, Universality: Contemporary Dialogues on the Left*. London:Verso.
LACLAU, E. (2004). Glimpsing the Future. In CRITCHLEY, S. and MARCHART, O. (eds.) *Laclau. A Critical Reader*. London and New York: Routledge.
LACLAU, E. (2005). *On Populist Reason*. London:Verso.
LACLAU, E. (2014). *The Rhetorical Foundations of Society*. London:Verso.
LACLAU, E. and MOUFFE, Ch. (1985). *Hegemony and Socialist Strategy. Towards a Radical Democratic Politics*. London:Verso.
MASSCHELEIN, J. and SIMONS, M. (2013a). The Politics of the University: Movements of (de-)Identification and the Invention of Public Pedagogic Forms. In SZKUDLAREK, T. (ed.) *Education and the Political. New Theoretical Articulations*. Rotterdam, Boston and Taipei: Sense Publishers.
MILERSKI, B. (2003), Pedagogika kultury. In KWIECIŃSKI, Z. and ŚLIWERSKI, B. (eds.) *Pedagogika, Podręcznik akademicki*. Warszawa: PWN.
OBUCHOWSKI, K. (1970). *Kody orientacji i struktura procesów emocjonalnych*. Warszawa: PWN.
PARKER, P. (1990). Metaphor and Catachresis. In BENDER, J. and WELLBERY, D.E. (eds.) *The Ends of Rhetoric. History, Theory, Practice*. Stanford: Stanford University Press.
ROUSSEAU, J.-J. (1921). *Emile, or Education*. [Online] Library of Liberty Project. Available from: http://lf-oll.s3.amazonaws.com/titles/2256/Rousseau_1499_EBk_v6.0.pdf. [Accessed: 15th September 2015].
ROUSSEAU, J.-J. (1923). *The Social Contract and Discourses by Jean-Jacques Rousseau* [Online]. Library of Liberty Project. Available from: http://oll.libertyfund.org/titles/638#lf0132_head_055. [Accessed: 20th December 2015].
SPRANGER, E. (1928). *Types of Men*. New York: G.E. Styrechert Company.
SZKUDLAREK, T. (2007). Empty Signifiers, Politics and Education. *Studies in Philosophy and Education*, 26 (3), pp. 237–252.
SZKUDLAREK, T. (2008). *Structure and Contents. Laclau, Populism and Cultural Pedagogy*. Paper to the Symposium *Facing Democratic Tensions in / through Education. New Educational Perspectives on Conflict and Culture*. [Online] Eskilstuna, https://www.researchgate.net/profile/Tomasz_Szkudlarek/contributions. [Accessed: 14th January 2016].
SZKUDLAREK, T. (2011). Semiotics of Identity. Education and Politics. *Studies in Philosophy and Education*, 30 (2), pp. 113–125.
SZKUDLAREK, T. (2013). Identity and Normativity: Politics and Education. In SZKUDLAREK, T. (ed.) *Education and the Political. New Theoretical Articulations*. Rotterdam, Boston and Taipei: Sense Publishers.
ŽIŽEK, S. (1989). *The Sublime Object of Ideology*. London:Verso.
ŽIŽEK, S. (1994). Identity and Its Vicissitudes: Hegel's "Logic of Essence" as Theory of Ideology. In LACLAU, E. (ed.) *The Making of Political Identities*. London:Verso.
ŽIŽEK, S. (2008). *In Defence of Lost Causes*. London:Verso.

Chapter 7

Theory, identity, and rhetorics
Summary and discussion

The connections between educational theories and the political are investigated in this book differently from approaches typical of educational research. Usually, we imply that theories have a mediated, indirect impact on social realities, i.e., they can influence them by being implemented in given domains of professional practice. Conversely, the way that political systems make their mark on the ways we think and write about education has also been the subject of scholarly inquiry. Both these ways of investigating the relations between education and politics are important; in my investigation, however, I connect educational theories, as instances of public discourse, with the discursive construction of political realities. This is where I localize the politics of theory. Following Ernesto Laclau, I assume that societies gain their identities, their historically specific "closures," by discursive and, especially, rhetorical means, and this is why my interpretations focus not only on the conceptual structures of theories, but also, and foremost, on the role of rhetorical figures and strategies.

The material presented in the preceding chapters is extensive, and I cannot recapitulate all the findings and partial interpretations here. Therefore, I have selected certain topics that prove to be structurally important, and I present them briefly here to make it easier to propose a hypothetical outline of the political rhetoric of educational theory. While the preceding chapters were organized around specific historical cases of theorizing education, in this chapter I detach their rhetorical elements and arrange them along a suggested meta-theoretical structure, comprising three of the threads identified in previous chapters, which create a tapestry into which other threads can be interwoven.

In Chapter 1, I mention two theoretical perspectives which influence my analytical strategy. The first is the Foucauldian and Rancièrean understandings of political power, which expose instances of discourse, knowledge, and the distribution of visibility (or "the sensible" in the more general approach proposed by Rancière). Following its Greek etymology, I understand theory as the organization of seeing, which permits addressing it both as discourse in Foucault's sense and as political in the sense proposed by Rancière. The second is Laclau's theory of the rhetorical construction of political identities. The key role is played here by the sequence of metonymies, metaphors/catachreses, empty signifiers, and synecdoches/hegemonies, which jointly define the steps leading from scattered and incommensurable demands to the provisional (and always "failed") totality. My assumption is that the way we make theories of education, or more exactly, how we employ linguistic resources to create their objects and to connect them into meaningful complexes, plays a significant role in this transition. More specifically, I assume that the discursive means applied in educational theories are, at the same time, elements of political ontologies, and that it is difficult for the political discourse to produce them without educational discourse.

These two themes (i.e., visibility/invisibility and totality) provide the groundwork from which other topics, tropes, and strategies are read as contributing to the creation of the political. The third element of this groundwork was not assumed at the beginning of my analyses, even though it can be elicited from Rancière's works. The theme of temporality, which proves indispensable in interpreting theories, cannot be subsumed to either of the two elements mentioned above. Other rhetorical devices and strategies, often decisive of the specificity of particular theories, are more or less functional in relation to these three basic strategies, i.e., to the construction of visibility/invisibility, to the tropological construction of totality, and to the construction of temporality. To some extent, visibility/invisibility and temporality, apart from being two of the pillars of the political rhetorics of education, are also functional with regard to the construction of totality.

Visibility, invisibility

The importance of the distinction between visibility and invisibility as the ontological condition of pedagogical agency, and of the effective construction of political singularity, is evident in the theories analyzed in this book. It is most overt in Rousseau's work. The style of his writing permits shifting between theoretical and meta-theoretical registers within the same text, which makes its ontological assumptions exceptionally transparent. The force constitutive of the ontological, determining the conditions for the construction of collective and individual identities, must operate within the invisible. This splits Rousseau's theory along the lines of the ontic and the ontological, into advice given to parents, teachers, and legislators, on the one hand, and into considerations regarding the very possibility of construing individualities and polities, on the other. This split repeats itself in the figures of teachers and legislators (see the comments on divinity further in this chapter), whose work is done partially as visible and – in its constitutive, ontological aspects – invisible to the subjects. One should note in this context that what critical theory laboriously *discovers* behind the curtains of social realities, i.e., that they are politically constructed veils of power relations or of "active forces" in Nietzschean/Deleuzian language, is *overtly* represented in Rousseau's treatises. To recall Harvey Mansfield's words, "one of Rousseau's techniques for concealing something is that of making it obvious and (for most readers) invisible" (Rousseau 1972, p. xxix). This may illustrate what I meant by making the very *difference* between visibility and invisibility invisible as functional to the logic of modern power (see Chapter 2).

Transforming knowledge of education into the science of education (see Chapter 3) adds another dimension to the operation of invisibility. To recall Gilles Deleuze's (2006) discussion about the Nietzschean understanding of force, it is only reactions to force that are experienced consciously by human beings. Following the trace of reactionality, science (in its positivistic variety) makes itself incapable of investigating the original, active forces that cause empirically accessible reactions. Herbart's insistence that the knowledge of education emulates the method of natural sciences, which is productive of mechanical models of learning and teaching, makes general pedagogy unable to analyze the operation of discipline within its conceptual logic. Discipline must be described metaphorically ("as if" it were a fluid medium). Thus, it is introduced into the theory as a significant factor in turning the chaotic and plural into the orderly and singular, but it is introduced as an object that cannot be described in a scientific way; its fluidity evades the mechanical language of the theory. In the long run, the failure of Herbart's science of education to subordinate the knowledge of education to the method borrowed from natural sciences can result from the impossibility of denouncing investigations into the invisible as unscientific. To some degree, this may be the result of the unceasing presence of the earlier work of Rousseau in the canon of pedagogical literature. Reading Rousseau makes one aware that the language of educational theory which overtly resorts to rhetorical figures is richer, and, in some respects, more *precise*, in addressing ontological issues than that coined on the model of physics or mathematics. In order to address social ontology, Herbart himself resorts to the idealistic language of ethics and to metaphors, thus instilling limits of explicability into his own doctrine.

The issue of postulational rhetoric (in the sense of postulating which stresses the making of demands rather than assuming truth, although both meanings are operative here – see the status of values in Chapter 6) should be recalled in this context. It is visible in the notorious use of "should" statements. This rhetoric is unavoidable in a discipline grounded in ethics: using "should" statements, one speaks of aims, which presupposes that something is valuable and that it does not exist. However, some "should" statements address issues that can also be addressed in the form of factual statements. If the object of the statement does exist, the "should" phrase invalidates its existence discursively; it turns it into a fictitious being that does not meet the criteria of true existence, or it makes it entirely invisible or unrecognizable. I discuss this issue in relation to the apparent existence of the socialist state (Chapter 4), but there is no doubt that it pertains to any polity built on ideological premises. In Chapter 5, I discuss the postulational rhetoric in the discourse of learning in the knowledge-based society, where the demands for building such societies through education and knowledge policies obliterate the fact that any society is a knowledge society, and, that as such, they are structured along the lines of the distribution of knowledge and ignorance. In short, knowledge capital depends on investments made both in knowledge and in ignorance, while the latter is barely visible behind the statements that we *should* build knowledge societies, which appear "good" by virtue of the positive connotations with the term "knowledge," and simply by the very fact of being demanded. Postulational rhetoric, in this case, strengthens the invisibility of exclusions made by the operation of the inclusive premises of the theory.

The last instance of invisibility I want to recall here is the epistemology of evasion. A brief description of it is provided in Chapter 4, where I treat it as correlative to the ontology of appearance. Quoting Staniszkis, who speaks of the "stubborn refusal" of the elites of socialist Poland to accept the fact that the society "is not what it is" in its conceptual logic, I speak of the epistemology of evasion as the organization of not knowing that maintains the apparent in its actual condition of incomprehensible reality. This issue cannot be developed within the limits of this book, but it is worth further elaboration. It speaks to the power of the commonplace, to the pedagogical/political circulation of *topoi*, to the fear of critical deconstruction of the given, to the feeling at home where one currently is in spite of the incompleteness or the absurdity of the situation. It refers to the ontic as "all there is," as Laclau (2005; 2000; 2004; 2014) often reminds us in his theory of the ontological. This issue opens up the fascinating terrain of empirical analyses that can shed more light on educational practice as constitutive both of *the police* and *politics* in Rancière's terms.

Risking a general remark, one may see the rhetoric of visibility and invisibility in education as a particular showcase of the modern instruments of control, where that which is made invisible as a policing strategy may be overtly visible as pedagogy; thus, it is strongly associated with childhood, immaturity, and other forms of the "not-yet" existence, and, by means of such infantilization, it becomes immunized against also being recognized as pertinent to adult citizens.

Instances of totality

The second important dimension of theories analyzed here is that of the construction of totality. It appears in several versions: as the need for restoring social singularity; as the demand for a strong moral character in the child, which is to guarantee his autonomy, or as the natural integrity of the child; as the creation of body politic and the construction of nations according to their nature; as traces of the divine; as the totality of educating society; and as the all-encompassing utopia of learning. Assuming, as Laclau has it, that social totality is ontologically impossible, which, in terms of his theory, means that it is provisional and cannot be accomplished by logical means, all these projects require tropological constructions. In this section, I reiterate some of these appearances of totality focusing on the notions of political singularity and divinity, and, second, I return to the work of tropes employed in their construction.

Political singularity

In Rousseau, singularity is always related to the plural and the fractional. The natural man, also in its incarnation in the body of Emile, is characterized by integrity and singularity ("he is the unit, the whole"), but in order to make him a citizen, he has to become "but the numerator of a fraction" (1921, p. 11). Civic education and the social contract must establish another singularity, that of the *body politic*, which is described by Rousseau as a "collective body" with "its unity, its common identity, its life and its will" (1923, p. 44). In *The Government of Poland* (1972), the circular play between the plural and the singular, encapsulating that between the natural and the construed, takes place within the body of the already existing nation. The nation has its nature, but this nature operates as the criterion of creating institutions that will *shape it* "accordingly to its nature."

In Herbart, the aim of education is the creation of the will and the strong moral character of the individual. Thus educated, the subject will be able to resist chaotic incentives and threatening forces, but first his aesthetic perceptions must be organized by the tutor in terms of their coherence, and then they undergo further systematization within the child's mind. The integration of the thus constructed subject with the social is guaranteed, first, by the operation of moral ideas which give the direction both to the individual will, and to the social body; and second, as Baker (2005) notes, by the operation of the same mechanical rules in the individual mind and in the "Newtonian" social space.

An important role is played in this context by the science of education, metaphorized by Herbart as a nation–state resisting foreign powers that threaten its independence. The science of education becomes, in fact, a sovereign agent of education; it speaks in the name of the universal and claims to incarnate the universal in the work of teachers and in the lives of their pupils. Its academic sovereignty is established as symmetrical to that designed for the child. The passage from the chaotic and inconsistent to the singular and persistent, from reactivity to character, both in the child and in general pedagogy, is made possible through the operation of discipline, working "as if" it was a fluid, hardly perceptible medium. The *fluidity* of this fluid metaphor of discipline, its detachment from conceptual hierarchies and mechanical explanations which comprise the core of Herbart's general pedagogy, is the hydraulic clutch by which Herbart's mechanics of education and the Benthamian/Foucauldian optics of control can operate jointly in the construction of the modern world.

This inability of the scientific language of education (as well as of psychology or sociology) to embrace the fluid logic of modern disciplinary power directly may be functional to the construction of the sovereignty of the abstract, formal, impersonal state. Their inclination to hierarchic, causal explanation invites an empty, fictitious "top" location from which the rationality of disciplinary power can emanate, from where something like the "Agent A" described in Chapter 3 – a hypostasis of the state, the society, or the Supersystem – can oversee the panoptic arrangement of the world. The pedagogy of educating society presented in Chapter 4 is an example of how such an instance of singularity, a substantiation of discipline in an all-encompassing supersystem controlling the particular milieus of education and socialization, can be construed as an empty signifier of the transcendent agent of ultimate control. Not only does its sanctified image permit the articulation of all aspects of social life into one political body, but it is endowed with fictitious, ultimate political agency as well. Such a mystic logic extends to present versions of political singularity. It certainly appears in the construction of the political body of the knowledge-based society.

As long as modern education can be described as the spacetime within which the social and the individual define their complex, mutual relations, this spacetime disintegrates in neoliberal logic. If we recall that, in spatial terms, the agora – the site where democracy was practiced in ancient times – was identical with the market place, we have to note that the contemporary market space is inhospitable to political participation, if it does not, in fact, render it impossible. With the lack of comprehensible connections between the individual and the construction of space in which the contemporary world acquires its shape, i.e., with the impotence of local citizenship and the impossibility of global citizenship, modern education faces its fundamental crisis. Referring to Bernadette Baker's observation that modern states can be explained as "systems of relations and methods of getting things done" (Baker 2005, p. 55), I note in Chapter 3 that among these "things" there is *the Thing* to be done – the very identity of the social – and that this function has always been present in the construction of modern education. In its neoliberal variety, the Thing is believed to be immanent: it construes itself, its quasi-biological, zoetic logic of economic mutations, competition, and selections seems to need only one output from its educational institutions: diversified, detached, movable humans whose skills in non-systematic thinking (labeled as creativity) will intensify mutation. Some of these mutations will win over others, and, thus, some world will crystallize. The space of the global economy is not a political space, not in the sense known from modernity. It appears to be an autopoietic immanence that constructs and reconstructs itself. Borrowing from Baker again, if the foundational metaphor of the modern pedagogical-political connectedness is Newtonian physics, and if the contemporary world cannot be described in such a Newtonian way any more, but instead it permits chaotic, zoetic, autopoietic, immanent, Deleuzian and otherwise non-linear and non-mechanical metaphors, we need to give these new metaphors both pedagogical and political significance; we need to re-think the ontology of the social, in its global scale, as simultaneously pedagogical and political.[1]

SUBJECTIVITY

Even though the construction of the subject is unquestionably the foundation of educational thinking, indeed its *raison d'être*, the four cases of educational theory discussed in this book provide us with radically different images of what, or who, the subject of education is. If we follow Osterwalder, Tröhler, and other thinkers who see education as the transformation of religion (see Chapter 2), the first instance of subjectivity is the human soul, and the aim of education is its salvation, or redemption. This notion is both continued and challenged by Rousseau, who situates the goodness of the child at the moment of birth rather than christening, which breaks the bonds with institutional churches; the child is good by nature rather than thanks to her admission into the ecclesiastical body. In short, Rousseau's subject is natural, but that naturalness is forgotten and has to be revived (and supplemented) in the course of education, which may succeed if it is based on that forgotten naturalness that must be implied, rather than recognized, as the foundation of upbringing. As I argue in the concluding part of this chapter, the status of nature in Rousseau is similar to that of equity in Rancière; it is a "presumptive tautology" that must be *made* true. We must remember that in the course of civic education, naturalness, and, with it, the singularity of the child, must be destroyed and turned into a fractional subjectivity if the social contract is to be made possible. It will return if the subject accepts all that has been done to him, when his apparently natural experiences were staged for him by the teacher (which Emile does in a quite Hegelian gesture of syntheses – "I have decided to be what you made me"), and in the construction of the nation.

In Herbart, the child has no natural goodness; he is an empty form to be filled by properly organized perceptions. In other words, the singularity of the subject is the function of aesthetics, which, in turn, depends on the pedagogical construction of attention, interests, the will, and character. Thus equipped, the subject is capable of organizing the world into a coherent, operative structure capable of creating new representations and of making him free – in the sense of being able to resist that which could distract him from the decisions of his will. In short, it depends not only on intellectual capabilities which determine the possibility of assimilating subsequent perceptions into the apperceptive masses, and their being productive of new ideas, but also on the strength of discipline which creates the basic conditions for the world to present itself as aesthetically organized.

In the case of the socialist pedagogy of educating society, which seems to have to do with an almost direct return of the mystic, religious discourse of subjectivity, socialism, which is equal to educating society, is to redeem fractured, alienated subjects. It incorporates them into the all-inclusive system in which contradictions disappear, and no force is needed to subordinate the will of the subjects to the common will of the polity. Everything is to be attained through education; this time it is evenly and imperceptibly dissolved in the tissues of the social. In a way, this doctrine continues the Herbartian concern with aesthetics, but in the social, rather than in the individual, domain. All pedagogically significant experiences must be coordinated (cf. the role of the school as the hub in which all formative experiences intersect and can be rationally distributed), and an educating totality of both free and fully united subjects – the real off-spring of the communist ideal as the transformation of the divine kingdom on Earth – can be attained. As I point out in Chapter 5, some features of this doctrine can be recognized in the contemporary discourse of learning in the knowledge-based society.

However, in the latter case we encounter not only the great *communitas* of learning, where all conflicts and antagonisms give way to the power of knowledge, but also the return of the fractional subject. The element which is silent in this educational utopia, while it is overtly present in its political and economical associates, is capital; the knowledge society is a capitalist society, and knowledge that "counts" is that which counts literally, i.e., that which can be turned into an economic asset giving its possessors financial advantage over those who are excluded from knowing. As I say in Chapter 5, the self-inclusive, immanent economy of global markets does not need *integrated*, self-directed subjects. It does not need *individuals*. On the contrary, what counts are only fractions and fragments of human bodies and souls. As the commonplace wisdom reflects in its metonymic codes, it was "hands" that mattered in the former types of capital, and it is "heads" that are hunted now. Instead of *individuals* (i.e., those who cannot be divided, the singular and the complete at the same time and in the same location), we are turned into *dividuals* (Deleuze 1990) – into fractured bodies and fractional skills that can belong to different data banks and be utilized by different corporate bodies for different purposes at the same time and in different spaces at once.

Divinity

As Daniel Tröhler (2014) puts it, the modern theory of education still remains, with its basic problems and solutions, within Protestant theology. John T. Scott (1994) speaks similarly about Rousseau's political theory, which he calls "the imitation of the divine." However, reading Rousseau, one can note significant ruptures and displacements within such religious connotations. As Osterwalder (2012) observes, the foundational concept of the origins of the goodness of the child in Rousseau is displaced from the act of christening to the moment of birth; Rousseau's child is *good by nature*. This gesture divorces education from the church and makes the child a sanctified being who needs to be read like the divine book of nature. The teacher also operates within a religious scenario. Similarly to the work of the legislator in *The Social Contract*, his work is "the imitation of the divine." Teachers and legislators, thus, are constructed as semigodly beings who do their invisible, creative job before the activities of common people are undertaken, as if creating the world before the arrival of man. The complexity of the modern project, on the one hand, implying universal human rights, and, on the other, treating society as an object of planned interventions executed by those capable of rational thinking, results in manipulation and deception in relation to the subjects endowed with such rights. The agency of educationalists and politicians splits here along the lines of the visible and the invisible, which corresponds to the split between the ontological and the ontic, as well as the ethical and the normative, as defined by Laclau. This split repeats, in a profane and displaced manner, the duality of the figure of Christ the Savior; teachers and legislators are both human and superhuman beings.

The divine also appears in later versions of educational theory. It is present in the transformed conception of the soul in Pestalozzi, in Herbart, in Humboldt, and in other "founding fathers" of educational theory; each of them, as Tröhler (2014) notes, was either a religious minister or the son of a religious minister. Following Tröhler, the differences in theoretical articulations between French and Swiss thinkers, on the one hand, and the German, on the other, corresponds to the distinction between the Calvinist and the Lutheran approach to the human soul – in brief, to the need for the purification of the soul in order to be a good citizen of one's own community (as in Pestalozzi), or to the need for inward freedom and fulfillment which makes one capable of living anywhere and maintaining a degree of independence from social constraints and seductions (as in Herbart). In later articulations, the sacred takes the form of values, of a political utopia (socialism, the educating society, the learning society), or of populist demands for a fully reconciled society as analyzed by Laclau. Spirituality is present and absent, or present *as* absent, in a displaced and diversely masked form, in all educational theories and ideologies (Znaniecka 2016). It is worth recalling here that François Tochon (2002) identifies priesthood as one of the three persistent tropics of teaching. In this context, the pedagogical appropriation of religious language, guided by the need for educationalizing the world (Smyers and Depaepe 2008) in order to transform it without resorting to revolutionary means, was an overall *profanation* of the human, the divine, and the social both in the sense proposed by Giorgio Agamben (2007), i.e., as returning the sacred (and, thus, inaccessible) to the "common use of men" (p. 73), and in a more common sense, as a blasphemous gesture of abuse. Acting educationally and politically, we can change people and societies. Such changes, however, concern conscious subjects, who can resist them; to be effective, they must resort occasionally to hidden strategies and manipulations. One could say that the very need for political and pedagogical effectiveness, thus, creates instances of *transcendence*; it splits the world of the subjects of education and political control into the spheres of the perceptible and the imperceptible, and it is the imperceptible that organizes the conditions of perceptibility. The sanctified, the invisible world of the *actors* of political and pedagogical control, of teachers and legislators, has its transcendence as well; it has to fear and respect *their* deities. These are the children and the people. The child and the people are both sanctified and profaned. This is why, as I show in my analysis of Rousseau, when acting pedagogically, we are operating on the threshold of guilt.

Such technical and normative complexity must produce complex and precise technologies of managing the known, the visible, the audible; Jacques Rancière (2011) encapsulates these spheres with the term of *the sensible*. Before I turn to

Rancière, I need to return to the tropologies involved in the construction of totality in a more systematic way, and, after that, to the temporal dimension of educational rhetorics.

Tropologies, theories, and totalities

Speaking figuratively, theories operate on territories populated by signs and objects which are connectible, and which can be articulated, classified, and interrelated. Metonymic contiguity is the most rudimentary condition of such elements to be considered for inclusion in the field of theorization. Other objects can be included later on the grounds of conceptual inferences and empirically identified relations. This means that the first gesture of construing a theory should make use of the contiguities that already exist – as stipulated either by cultural codes, in Eco's terms, or by the material relations between the objects. Some of such prior contiguities may not appear in the content of theory other than as its background, as its material and cultural condition of possibility. However, in order to fulfill the claims of novelty and explanatory power, the theory should re-articulate such contiguities and attract new elements to the field. In the latter case, the process of *construing* contiguities – or chains of equivalence, in Laclau's language – must be overtly present in its body.

Such a dual presence of metonymy, i.e., as the condition of delineating the field of the theory, and as a figure in the content of the theory that makes it coherent and expansible, can be illustrated in the discourse of education in the knowledge-based society (Chapter 5). In its background, there is an apparently neutral observation that in contemporary societies meanings become important as elements of production strategies and culture becomes a commodity. This points to a metonymic contiguity, but – and this is where metaphorization, and, with it, a theoretical structure begins – it is quickly turned into a bi-directional coupling (in Carusi's terms 2011), in which culture is *identified* as the production of commodities, while such production is *grounded* in culture. The same coupling arrives in the discourse of education. It allows for the broadening of the field of educational knowledge by articulating it metonymically with investment policies, international competition, cost reductions, employability, etc., and, against this background, for developing "metaphorical" strategies of managing culture and education *as* the production of human capital. Educational strategies circulate this metaphor in endless repetitions, which establishes it as a catachresis; the coupling ceases to be seen as metaphorical. Then come practical implementations: of training creative skills, of producing effective knowledge workers, of making human capital employable on global markets. The material practices initiated thus create experiential referents for this figure; they turn it into a catachresis and make it operate like a quasi-concept. The theory acquires its descriptive truth value.

While the initial metonymical connectivity of elements, permitted by cultural codes and by particular material relations, does not need theoretical justification, the process of expanding such connections and creating the explanatory potential of theory demands that the creation of contiguities be visible. In Delors's report (1996), the emerging theory of learning expands its field, articulating new elements and defining a horizon in which they can be made contiguous (this expansion can be described as the learnification of education – Biesta 2012). In Laclau's words, this is the moment of creating equivalence and of the construction of catachreses as a condition of reconstructing the discursive field under a new signifier of totality. Learning is claimed to overcome the tensions between the global and the local, the universal and the individual, between tradition and modernity, long-term and short-term considerations, between competition and equality of opportunities, between the expansion of knowledge and the limited capacities of its being absorbed by individuals, and between the material and the spiritual. The articulation of these tendencies in one field resorts to two integrating instances appearing simultaneously in the text. As Delors puts it, the prospects of the (then) coming twenty-first century evoke "anguish and hope" (p. 14), and the text follows these two traits in its argumentation. The "necessary utopia" of learning is to reduce the former and promote the latter. The constitutive outside is created by excluding those tendencies which lead to "poverty, exclusion, ignorance, oppression and war" (p. 13), which, in turn, helps to integrate the incommensurable positive demands in one chain (or plane) of equivalence. However, the articulation of these antagonisms, and the way learning is described in this context, clearly foretell exclusions that will be made in the name of this empty signifier. In the offspring discourse of education in the knowledge-based society, such exclusions are explicit, and they oscillate around the issue of ignorance management.

An important role in defining the terrain in which heterogeneous elements can be articulated is played by the act of enclosure. Herbart's general pedagogy, metaphorized as a nation-state with a distinctive culture and protected borders, excludes stranger languages from its field. This exclusion creates conditions for creating a cultural code necessary for the construction of relevant contiguities, and, thus, for the identification of objects which can become the subject of the science of education. These objects are dissociated from the languages of philosophy, medicine, or theology, and are made ready for their re-articulation as pedagogical. The construction of the psychological mechanics of the mind, and of a symmetrical technology of instruction, would not be possible without that founding gesture of bordering the language of education against other languages.

However, in all the theories analyzed here, the borders of educational discourse provide for numerous passages to the political. Apart from Herbart's physics, which couples education and psychology, on the one hand, and education and politics, on the other, I pointed to the bi-directional work of nature in Rousseau (education is to be natural, but the nature of children and nations must be revealed through education), to the notion of educating society in the Polish discourse of socialist education (educating society is socialism, and socialism demands the construction of educating society), and to the coupling of economy and education in the discourse of learning in the knowledge-based society. Initially, such passages have the structure of copular metaphors. In other words, the fields of education and politics are kept as semantically separate, but they are bi-directionally coupled in the relations of identification and grounding (Carusi 2011). A series of particular metaphors operates within this general construction of connections between politics and education. In Chapter 2, for instance, I speak of how the proclamation of strangeness of Poland leads to the infantilization of the country, to its identification with that which is natural in European nations, and, by grounding politics in education, to treating the formation of nations like the education of children.

How do such metaphors turn into catachreses? First, by iterations, which gradually turn them into "dead metaphors." Second, educational theories have the potential of being turned into policies (or, in fact, it is policies that frequently play the role of theories nowadays), and, as such, are capable of creating material referents to their metaphors. The metaphor which states that education is business makes educational actors behave accordingly, and soon it points to certain material practices (like the distribution of money to competing schools on the basis of their test scores), and, thus, it becomes a quasi-concept, a catachresis.

Another aspect of the operation of catachreses central to Laclau's theory is that they are empty signifiers that, unlike the ones that point to objects and practices materialized in educational policies, denote impossible social totality (see Chapter 6). Their work is that of integrating the heterogeneous elements of a given field by way of *naming* the field as a totality, which involves a synecdochal elevation of a particular term "to the dignity of the Thing" (Laclau 2005). The theories discussed include, for instance, signifiers of the knowledge-based society and the educating society, notions of nature and the nation in Rousseau, and the synecdochal construction of teaching and the teacher in Herbart, where they represent the universal dimension of the society, or the State. As I note in Chapter 6, the discursive operations of the theory of education in this respect are doubled by educational practices. Theories postulate that education should be grounded in certain values (like liberty, autonomy, nature, justice, etc.) and associate such values with certain political and cultural settings. The daily work of construing personal and collective identities demands that the terms of values are constantly circulated not only in theoretical debates, but also in curricular practice; that they become complex through endless exemplary applications, that they are kept open and vague, and that their significance is nearly sacred. Schools are factories of empty signifiers, and, like theories, they are *excessive* in their work; they produce more empty terms than are demanded in current political contexts, and, thus, they contribute to the creation and maintenance of cultural repositories of empty signifiers applicable in the construction of "possible impossible totalities."

To conclude, the tropological structure constitutive of the political in Laclau's theory is fully present in theories of education. However, as I note in Chapter 6, its interpretation must take into account that the signifiers of totalizing identity are purposefully construed in education, while in Laclau's analyses they emerge somewhat spontaneously in synecdochal investments of the universal into the particular.[2] Moreover, educational practices create normative milieus which can be different from common rules and regulations, which means that the language of education must address ethical issues differently from that of politics. These two features of education point to its reconstructive, political function, to its role in creating the sphere of possibility for the political.

Temporality

The last element constitutive to the rhetorical structure of educational theory to be reiterated here concerns the construction of temporality. It appears in previous chapters more incidentally than those reported above; nevertheless, it is one of the fundamental rhetorical structures in theorizing education and also in its connections to the political. An example is the inconsistency in how education is understood in *Emile* and in *The Social Contract*, which disappears when education is read as diversified in time or as sequential. The child is born good by nature and as a unitary subject. First, education is meant to reveal that natural integrity. *Then* the integrity is destroyed by education aimed at the construction of a "fractional subject," whose integrity depends on belonging to a larger body politic. Once this new collective body is established and singularity is regained, nature returns as a feature of nations. It is made of their histories and the habits acquired or inculcated in the process of them *becoming* singular. From this point, their education has to be organized by institutions "pertinent to their nature" and capable of revealing that nature – nations are brought up like children (Szkudlarek 2005). Thus, nations are described as autopoietic entities, immanent in their process of *becoming what they are* and sustaining that "what" in iterative processes of construing their political and human bodies.

Another specific instance of temporality is that of the *not-yet*. It speaks to the utopian dimension of educational and political thinking, in which the truly complete (identity, totality, personal autonomy, a fully reconciled society) is delegated to the future and education is believed to adapt individuals to such ideal, not-yet existing forms of the social, while politics claims to be capable of materializing such ideal forms. Politics and education operate in the domain of *becoming* rather than in the factuality of what there is. This orientation is productive of several other rhetorical strategies. One is that of *temporal encroachment*, which operates on the singularity, fragmentation, totality, and plurality mentioned above. It also refers to the mutations of divinity in pedagogical and political discourse, where teachers and legislators create future realities for their subjects by means of pre-organizing their worlds of experience, such that they take them for granted as "natural." In other words, temporal encroachment depends on controlling the past in order to create the future, which allows the masters of such operations to distance themselves from direct interventions into thus pre-organized, apparently "natural" experiences.

Another element with a strong temporal aspect is postulational rhetoric. In its operation of bypassing the present, it is similar to the work of temporal encroachments. Let us recall that this rhetoric operates through "should" statements, and, inevitable as it is as an element of the temporal/utopian dimension of education, it also has the power to invalidate discursively the existing objects it is applied to; they are not "true enough" to count pedagogically or politically, their work is insignificant, they are thus made invisible and can be utilized in power relations.

In structural terms, the topos of educational temporality, in all its instances, is grounded in Christian eschatology. The sequence of integrity, fragmentation, and the reconstruction of integrity in a new body, in a *communion* which transcends both the primary singularity and its subsequent fragmentation, reflects the history of salvation.

This brief overview of themes, figures, and strategies operational in theories of education cannot be complete. My intention here is merely to underline the structure built around the topics of visibility/invisibility, totality, and temporality, and of the tropologies and strategies engaged in their construction that organize the rhetorical dimension of the theories of education discussed in this book. To conclude this recapitulation of the political rhetorics of educational theories, I want to place them in the context of an overview of political rhetoric, as such, provided by Susan Condor, Cristian Tileagă, and Michael Billig (2013). The authors do not treat political rhetoric in ontological terms, but rather as instruments of persuasion in effective political campaigns. Nevertheless, their overview includes the rhetorical construction of identity. Identity, or "projected commonality between the speaker and audience" (p. 277) is merely an instrument of effective persuasion, but one must note that such "commonalities" live longer than do acts of persuasion, and, thus, become elements of social objectivity. These rhetorics do not reflect Laclau's tropology directly, but they can easily be interpreted in such terms, and they correspond to the rhetorical dimensions of the theories discussed in this book. For instance, they include "explicit appeals to common in-group membership," which includes regrouping "a composite group into a single rhetorical entity" (p. 279) and "constructing aspirational identities," where "the object of political address (e.g., 'the nation') is projected into an undetermined future" (p. 280). Moreover, the notion of the "we" in such political strategies is described in terms of flexibility and vagueness, which evoke the notion of the empty signifier in Laclau. What this means for the interpretation proposed in this book is that, first, the content of the Laclauan perspective is not far from the content of traditional, instrumental political rhetoric. However, apart from being far more precise as to the tropological instruments applicable in the construction of identity, it treats identity seriously and responsibly and not as a mere provisional effect instrumental to the goals of particular campaigns, but as social objectivity, which, in spite of being construed in the course of historically specific mobilizations and manipulations, is absolutely real and is there to last for some time. Second, the links between current politics, current educational practices, and social objectivities can indeed be understood not only traditionally, as those that emphasize the influence of politics in educational practices, but also as those in which educational and political practices, with all their contextuality and provisionality, are constitutive of social objectivities.

Some of the results of my analyses invite a more direct reference to Jacques Rancière's theory. The final section of this chapter is devoted to this issue.

Engaging Rancière

A number of educational philosophers and theorists, such as Gert Biesta (2006; 2010a; 2010; 2013), Jan Masschelein and Maarten Simons (2011; 2013; 2013a), Carl-Anders Säfström (Biesta and Säfström 2011; Säfström 2013), Claudia Ruitenberg (2010; 2013), Tyson Lewis (2012), Charles Bingham (2010; Bingham and Biesta 2010), and others, refer to Rancière today in the search for fresh impulses to revitalize educational theory. Similar to the tendency of distinguishing between the ontic and the ontological in social analyses, these authors engage in defining "the educational" in education to revitalize the ontology of educating. This shared interest involves attempts to clear the concept of education of sedimented features that cover its specificity with endless secondary appearances. For instance, Biesta (2006) points to the function of subjectification, which is often equated with emancipation, as the only one that is educational *per se*, i.e., unlike the functions of qualification and socialization, it cannot be performed without specifically educational institutions or beyond specifically educational relations.

An important aspect of this ontology of education is *risk*, or the danger that education brings to the world of established practices, identifications, and institutions (Biesta 2013). Education brings risk because subjectification involves de-identification from the effects of socialization and contributes to the radical "beginning," or renewing, of the world with the arrival of every human subject as a unique being. Thus, education in its emancipatory function is ultimately radical, and, therefore, it is constantly *tamed*, as Masschelein and Simons (2013) say, by unceasing efforts to make it predictable, controllable, and safe for the world in its present shape. Taming refers to both the school (by its politicization, pedagogization, naturalization, technologization, psychologization, or popularization) and the teacher (by her professionalization or flexibilization). In its generic meaning revitalized by these authors, the school (*scholé*) is a disruptive space and free time – a place and a time where everything can begin, where children are dissociated from their families and communities, and where they interact with teachers and other students around specific objects of their interest and around things and issues that are "put on the table" just because of that interest. This is why, as functional to the becoming of the unknown, it is being reduced to the various forms of the known, familiar, and predictable.

Thus understood, in its disruptive and tamed activities, the school is situated in the "slash" of the ontic/ontological distinction, which, as Biesta and Säfström (2011) put it, is the position between "what is" and "what is not." In Rancière's language, this position is that of dissensus, of disruptive politics which question the police order of that which is.

The most intensely debated Rancière work is, in this context, *The Ignorant Schoolmaster* (1991). Commenting on the pedagogy of a nineteenth-century teacher, Joseph Jacotot, Rancière insists that equity cannot be *arrived at* through education. Rather than working against inequality, Jacotot *assumes*, as the "presumptive tautology" (Bingham 2010), the equality of all intelligences: everyone is capable of mastering anything; they all succeeded in learning the most difficult thing, which is their mother tongue, and nothing more difficult will be demanded of them. The aim of teaching is to *verify* (in the sense of "making true," *veritas – facere*) this assumption. The assumption can be challenged easily as counter-factual, "[b]ut our problem isn't proving that all intelligences are equal. It's seeing what can be done under that supposition," writes Rancière (1991, p. 46). This is the only possibility for emancipation to happen. In other words, the best possible answer to the question what to do with inequalities is to *ignore them*, act as if they do not exist, assume that the students *can do it*, and see how far they can go. Also, do not explain anything; explication positions people as ignorant, and it makes them ignorant. The way Jacotot deals with this problem is through his own project of "universal teaching," which can be summarized as letting people learn on their own after providing them with skillfully chosen resources. Jacotot used a bilingual edition of *Télémach* (a novel by Fénelon) to teach French to Flemish students in a situation in which neither of the sides could speak the language of the other. The condition is that the teacher commands a certain authority and the students want to follow his recommendations as to what to do and how to do it. As Jacotot asserts, "man is a will served by intelligence" (Rancière 1991, p. 51–52), and this is why teaching is not the transmission of knowledge, but the direct relation of will to will, intelligence to intelligence.

Jacotot's case is used by Rancière to support his previous claim that emancipation is possible only as an individual, disruptive act. This argument appears, for instance, in *Proletarian Nights* (2012), where Rancière analyzes the histories of workers – socialist activists concerned with their personal emancipation, guided by their will to live as free people, to write poems, and to belong to artistic communities. The distribution of *time* proves the fundamental condition of being or not being free in this sense. Elsewhere (2011), Rancière reminds us that in Plato artisans were to be excluded from public activities as those who do not have time for it. This approach corresponds strictly to Rancière's understanding of politics that "happen" as a disruptive movement within police orders and as the reorganization of the distribution of the sensible. Intellectual emancipation, as in Jacotot's case, is, thus, possible not owing to institutional arrangements, but in spite of them. This is why contemporary pedagogical readings of Rancière are challenging to the understanding of education. In their concern with emancipation, it is as if the authors cited above strip the school of its institutional complexity and political complicity, and, in a gesture reminiscent of Rousseau's subtractive construction of nature, they reveal "the educational" in education: its power of dissociation, the suspension of the world outside, the total focus on the object put on the table. Rancière insists that institutional education cannot be emancipatory and that emancipation is impossible as social emancipation. This does not mean that one should not care about schools; schooling should be improved, just as much as policing should be made more human, as Bingham notes in his afterword to Rancière's (2010) revisiting of the issue of ignorance. However, as Biesta, Masschelein and Simons, and other thinkers of this orientation add, emancipation *happens* in schools, and schools are *proper* places for it to happen, but nowadays it happens as *disruptive* to their order rather than as a result of that order. As Biesta and Säfström insist, it also happens as disruptive to specific educational temporality. Referring to his and C. A. Säfström's thesis that education is positioned between "what is" and "what is not," (Biesta and Säfström 2011), Biesta says that "the most common reading of this tension is one where the 'what is not' is understood in temporal terms, that is as 'what is not *yet*'"(Biesta 2013a, p. 76). Educational thinking is typically organized around the concepts of change, learning, development, progress, and the child as the bearers of that "not yet," linear temporality. In such a setting, freedom, which is what really matters in education, is at risk of being deferred forever. This is why Biesta and Säfström refer to the tension between what is and what is not as the Rancièrean dissensus, and Biesta follows this route by considering the possibility of thinking of education beyond the temporal scheme. While temporality may be indispensable to thinking about qualification and socialization, Biesta doubts whether it is the proper framework for the concern with subjectification. The possibility of "taking the time out" of education arrives when we assume that the child is a speaking subject. The speaking subject, or the child *assumed* as speaking (like a "babbling" infant), is here and now, and the relation with the child is not guided by the "not-yet"; the subject will not arrive in the future because he/she is right here now. This topic is continued by Säfström (2013) in his vision of class as "the community of poets." In brief, if the educational of education is concerned with freedom and subjectivity, it is not temporal; education concerned with subjectivity dwells in the sphere of possibility, in the tension between "is" and "is not," in dissensus, rather than between "is" and "is not yet."

The way I refer to Rancière in this book assumes a different focus. My intention is not to sieve the educational out from the numerous functions and roles education currently plays, but rather to identify the work of the political within some exemplary instances of educational theory. In what way is this analysis Rancièrean?

First, I want to note that Rancière's reading of Joseph Jacotot's work recalls some of the features I discuss in the chapters devoted to Rousseau and Herbart. Clearly, Jacotot speaks from the perspective of his time, and some of his ideas are less unique in relation to those of other intellectuals than Rancière's analysis suggests by singling Jacotot out from the context of the educational thought of the epoch. The way I read it, the radical "presumptive tautology" of Jacotot's/Rancière's equity is no less radical than Rousseau's assumption of the natural goodness of man. The maxim "All men are good by nature" challenges the moral and religious foundations of inequality and disrupts the power of the Church as the provider of morality. It opens the way to the dream of a republican society in which every subject is a citizen equal to others. Moreover, the idea of the *verification* of such an easily questionable assumption is also strongly present in Rousseau, albeit not under the same name. Briefly, natural goodness is *assumed* by Rousseau as the point of departure of societal order, and only if that order is construed *according* to that assumption, will goodness reveal itself in actuality. By the way, such "presumptive tautology" seems to be characteristic of educational theories, if not of social theories in general. Such theories can start with utopian fantasies or with abstract ideals. If they inspire some social action, they produce material referents to their signifiers, and are, thus, *verified* in the purely Rancièreian sense. In other words, it is not because they are true that they are implemented; *it is because they are implemented that they become true* (see Chapter 5). To some extent, this is a feature of science in general as well. At least in its experimental and technical aspects, science is capable of *creating* the objects of its investigation and appears no less radical in its "presumptive tautologies" than the Rancièrean assumption of equality.

Further, is Jacotot's assumption of equality indeed far more radical than Herbart's assumption of universal educability? How far is the claim that all children are educable from the claim that everybody can learn anything? We do not find the *argument* for the "presumptive tautology" of educability in Herbart's scientific discourse as we do in Rousseau and Jacotot; nor do we find the critique of explication here. However, when Herbart's theory becomes partially incarnated into the practice of teacher training for compulsory schooling, the tautological cycle reveals its logic here as well. To add another dimension of similarity, Herbart is quite "Jacototist" in his understanding of the will to will relation, and, thus, in his recognition of the role of authority.

To conclude, in discovering Jacotot Rancière describes quite a number of assumptions shared by other pedagogues of the time. The unquestionable difference is, though, that Rancière speaks against the idea of social emancipation, which is what we like to see as central to modern educational theory. In other words, I have been moving around topics similar to those discussed by Rancière, but not quite with the Rancièrean disruptive ontology in mind. My frame of reference is, in this respect, more that of Laclau's.

There is one more connection between my analyses of Herbart and Rancière's thought concerning the role of aesthetics, or the role of the organization of perceptions, as a condition of learning. The role of the government over children and of the fluid discipline can be seen in the same context; it is to organize the space of perceptions, reactions, and experience so that the child can be educated simultaneously as an individual and as a member of the community. It is necessary to recall Rancière's notion of aesthetics and his concept of the distribution of the sensible here. Rancière (2011, p. 10) describes aesthetics as "a mode of articulation between ways of doing and making, their corresponding forms of visibility, and possible ways of thinking about their relationships." He also adds a broader definition:

> aesthetics can be understood in a Kantian sense – re-examined perhaps by Foucault – as the system of *a priori* forms determining what presents itself to sense experience. It is a delimitation of spaces and times, of the visible and the invisible, of speech and noise, that simultaneously determines the place and the stakes of politics as a form of experience. Politics revolves around what is seen and what can be said about it, around who has the ability to see and the talent to speak, around the properties of spaces and the possibilities of time.
>
> (2011, p. 13).

And, in this context, he defines the distribution of the sensible as:

> the system of self-evident facts of sense perception that simultaneously discloses the existence of something in common and the delimitations that define the respective parts and positions within it. . . . This apportionment of parts and positions is based on a distribution of spaces, times, and forms of activity that determines the very manner in which something in common lends itself to participation and in what way various individuals have a part in this distribution.
>
> (2011, p. 12)

How do these notions relate to the results of my analyses? Undoubtedly, we can see how educational theories are implicated in the distribution of the sensible, how their work contributes to the "distribution of spaces, times, and forms of activity," and how specific theoretical projects address, variably but continuously, the same project of *construing* "the a priori forms determining what presents itself to sense experience." What this connection suggests is that my interpretation reveals more of *the police* than of *politics* (in Rancière's terms). In other words, the political work of educational theories analyzed here is dominated by questions of connecting, totalizing, and harmonizing the social and the individual, rather than by those of disruptions, dissensus, and de-identification constitutive of individual emancipation and subjectification. By no means is this observation surprising or disquieting; it merely reflects the focus of my analyses. They are directed by the question of how the rhetoric of educational theory is constitutive of the political, and the totalizing aspect of the political simply appears to be at the foreground of these theories. Perhaps this systematizing bias is, simply, endemic to theory as the *organization* of seeing; perhaps disruptions and demonstrations of difference elude theorization; perhaps they can only be encouraged – but their execution cannot be "designed," because any design falls into the *logic* of the system. It is always tempting to write a theory against the power of theory, and the cases of Derrida and Rancière (and Rousseau as well) are beautiful examples of such deconstructive work. However, in the end of the day, it is always those who are *theorized* that have to disrupt the logics of the system, to claim their voice and their place *in spite* of the orders of the sensible, including theoretical ones. In fact, what else is Rancière telling us when he says, in his *theory*, that emancipation is possible only as an individual act?

However, nothing is complete. There are ruptures in theoretical logics which make room for political disruptions of seeing as well. Moreover, they are significant as elements of the politics of theory in education. In Chapter 1, I pointed to Robert Innis's observation that Rousseau foretells the idea of radical democracy, currently identified with Laclau and Mouffe, and this is indeed also close to Rancière's thought.[3] The gesture of distancing societal order from nature, in spite of its aura of lamentation, frees the social from any predefined constrains and makes it fully construable. Rousseau's "godly gestures" of inventing the foundations for natural education, social contract polities, and national identities, in spite of their totalizing ends, *are* ontologically disruptive. On the other hand, I have pointed to the *excess* of such totalizing devices in educational theories, and suggested that it is reflected, and intensified, in educational practice. Both theories and practices of education produce repositories of empty signifiers ("empty terms of values"), which are indispensable as rhetorical tools of political reconstructions. This element, as well as the overall rhetoricity of educational discourse, its saturation with tropes and *topoi* applicable in the construction and reconstructions of both individual and collective identity, of *any* identity, as Laclau insists, indeed situate the theory of education *in the space of possibility* between that which is and that which is not, between the police and politics, between the ethical and the normative, and between the ontic and the ontological. This is precisely where the theorists to whom I refer above situate education.

Notes

1   As this passage clearly shows, postulational rhetoric is indeed indispensable if one starts thinking pedagogically.
2   As I argue in Chapter 6, and more extensively in Szkudlarek (2011), this is not a universally valid observation. Such investments can be, and sometimes are, arranged in professionally staged campaigns.
3   For an analysis of the similarities and differences between Laclau and Rancière, see the final sections of Laclau's *On Populist Reason* (2005).

References

AGAMBEN, G. (2007). *Profanations*. New York: Zone Books.
BAKER, B. (2005). State-formation, Teaching Techniques, and Globalisation as Aporia. *Discourse: Studies in the Cultural Politics of Education*, 26 (1), pp. 45–77.

BIESTA, G. (2006). *Beyond Learning: Democratic Education for a Human Future.* Boulder and London: Paradigm.

BIESTA, G. (2010). *Good Education in the Time of Measurement. Ethics, Politics, Democracy.* Boulder and London: Paradigm.

BIESTA, G. (2012). Giving Teaching Back to Education: Responding to the Disappearance of the Teacher. *Phenomenology & Practice,* 6 (2), pp. 35–49.

BIESTA, G. (2013). *The Beautiful Risk of Education.* Boulder and London: Paradigm.

BIESTA, G. (2013a). Time Out: Can Education Do and Be Done Without Time? In SZKUDLAREK, T. (ed.) *Education and the Political. New Theoretical Articulations.* Rotterdam, Boston and Taipei: Sense Publishers.

BIESTA, G. and SÄFSTRÖM, C.A. (2011). A Manifesto for Education. *Policy Futures in Education,* 9 (5), pp. 540–547.

BINGHAM, Ch. (2010a). Under the Name of Method: On Jacques Rancière's Presumptive Tatutology. In RUITENBERG, C. (ed.) *What do Philosophers of Education do? (And How Do They Do It?).* Hoboken: Wiley-Blackwell.

BINGHAM, Ch. and BIESTA, G. (2010). *Jacques Rancière. Education, Truth, Emancipation.* Boulder and London: Paradigm.

CARUSI, F.A. (2011). *The Persistence of Policy: A Tropological Analysis of Contemporary Education Policy Discourse in the United States.* [Online] Scholar Works. Available from: http://scholarworks.gsu.edu/eps_diss/82/ [Accessed: 29th November 2015].

CONDOR, S., TILEAGĂ, C. and BILLIG, M. (2013). Political Rhetoric. In HUDDY, L., SEARS, D.O. and LEVY, J.S. (eds.) *The Oxford Handbook of Political Psychology (2 ed.).* Oxford: Oxford University Press.

DELEUZE, G. (1990). Society of Control. L'autre journal, No.1, Mai. [Online]: https://www.nadir.org/nadir/archiv/netzkritik/societyofcontrol.html. [Accessed: 18th March 2016].

DELEUZE, G. (2006), *Nietzsche and Philosophy.* Translated by Hugh Tomlinson with the foreword by Michael Hardt. New York: Columbia University Press.

DELORS, J. et al. (1996). *Learning: The Treasure within. Report to UNESCO of the International Commission on Education for the Twenty-first Century.* [Online] UNESCO Publishing. Available from: http://unesdoc.unesco.org/images/0010/001095/109590eo.pdf. [Accessed: 10th November 2015].

LACLAU, E. (2000). Identity and Hegemony: The Role of Universality in the Construction of Political Logic. In BUTLER, J., LACLAU, E. and ŽIŽEK, S. (eds.) *Contingency, Hegemony, Universality: Contemporary Dialogues on the Left.* London: Verso.

LACLAU, E. (2004). Glimpsing the future. In CRITCHLEY, S., MARCHART, O. (eds.) *Laclau. A critical reader.* London and New York: Routledge.

LACLAU, E. (2005). *On Populist Reason.* London: Verso.

LEWIS, T.E. (2012). *The Aesthetics of Education: Theatre, Curiosity, and Politics in the Work of Jacques Rancière and Paulo Freire.* London: Bloomsbury Publishing.

LACLAU, E. (2014). *The Rhetorical Foundations of Society.* London: Verso.

MASSCHELEIN, J. and SIMONS, M. (eds.) (2011). *Rancière, Public Education, and the Taming of Democracy.* Hoboken: Wiley-Blackwell.

MASSCHELEIN, J. and SIMONS, M. (2013). *In Defence of the School: A Public Issue.* Leuven: E-ducation, Culture & Society.

MASSCHELEIN, J. and SIMONS, M. (2013a). The Politics of the University: Movements of (de-)identification and the Invention of Public Pedagogic Forms. In SZKUDLAREK, T. (ed.) *Education and the Political. New Theoretical Articulations.* Rotterdam, Boston and Taipei: Sense Publishers.

OSTERWALDER, F. (2012). The Modern Religious Language of Education: Rousseau's Emile. *Studies in Philosophy and Education*, 31, pp. 432–447.

RANCIÈRE, J. (1991). *The Ignorant Schoolmaster. Five Lessons in Intellectual Emancipation.* Stanford: Stanford University Press.

RANCIÈRE, J. (2010). On Ignorant Schoolmasters. In Bingham, Ch. and Biesta, G. (eds.) *Jacques Rancie`re: Education, Truth, Emancipation.* London and New York: Continuum.

RANCIÈRE, J. (2011). *The Politics of Aesthetics. The Distribution of the Sensible.* London and New York: Continuum.

RANCIÈRE, J. (2012). *Proletarian Nights. The Workers' Dream in Nineteenth-Century France.* London: Verso.

ROUSSEAU, J.-J. (1921). Emile, or Education. [Online] Library of Liberty Project. Available from: http://lf-oll.s3.amazonaws.com/titles/2256/Rousseau_1499_EBk_v6.0.pdf. [Accessed: 15th September 2015].

ROUSSEAU, J.-J. (1923), The Social Contract and Discourses by Jean-Jacques Rousseau. [Online] Library of Liberty Project. Available from: http://oll.libertyfund.org/titles/638#lf0132_head_055. [Accessed: 15th August 2015].

ROUSSEAU, J.-J. (1972). The Government of Poland. Indianapolis: Bobbs-Merill. [Online]: International Relations and Security Network. Available from http://www.isn.ethz.ch/Digital-Library/Publications/Detail/?id=125482. [Accessed: 15th September 2015].

RUITENBERG, C. (2010). Conflict, Affect and the Political: On Disagreement and Democratic Capacity. *Factis Pax. Journal of Peace Education and Social Justice*, 4 (1), pp. 40–55.

RUITENBERG, C. (2013). The Double Subjectification Function of Education: Reconsidering Hospitality and Democracy. In SZKUDLAREK, T. (ed.) *Education and the Political. New Theoretical Articulations.* Rotterdam, Boston and Taipei: Sense Publishers.

SÄFSTRÖM, C.A. (2013). Stop Making Sense! And Hear the Wrong People Speak. In SZKUDLAREK, T. (ed.) *Education and the Political. New Theoretical Articulations.* Rotterdam, Boston and Taipei: Sense Publishers.

SCOTT, J. (1994). Politics as the Imitation of the Divine in Rousseau's Social Contract. *Polity*, XXVI (3), pp. 473–501.

SMYERS, P. and DEPAEPE, M. (eds.) (2008). *Educational Research: The Educationalization of Social Problems.* Dordrecht: Springer.

SZKUDLAREK, T. (2005). On nations and children: Rousseau, Poland, and European identity. *Studies in Philosophy and Education*, 24. pp. 19–38.

SZKUDLAREK, T. (2011). Semiotics of Identity. Education and Politics. *Studies in Philosophy and Education*, 30 (2), pp. 113–125.

TOCHON, F. (2002). *The Tropics of Teaching. Productivity, Warfare and Priesthood.* Toronto, Buffalo and London: University of Toronto Press.

TRÖHLER, D. (2014). Between Universally Claimed Theory and a Common Understanding: Theorhertical Knowledge in Education. In BIESTA, G., ALLAN, J. and EDWARDS, R. (eds.) *Making a Difference in Theory. The Theory Question in Education and the Education Question in Theory.* London and New York: Routledge.

ZNANIECKA, M. (2016). *Kategoria duchowości w pedagogice. Ślady obecności.* Doctoral thesis. University of Gdańsk.

Index